RELATING SUICIDE

Critical Interventions in the Medical and Health Humanities

Series Editors

Stuart Murray, Sowon Park, Corinne Saunders and Angela Woods

Critical Interventions in the Medical Humanities promotes a broad range of scholarly work across the Medical and Health Humanities, including both larger-scale intellectual projects and argument-led provocations, to present new field-defining, interdisciplinary research into health and human experience.

Titles in the series

Abortion Ecologies in Southern African Fiction, Caitlin E. Stobie
COVID-19 and Shame, Fred Cooper, Luna Dolezal and Arthur Rose
Relating Suicide, Anne Whitehead

Forthcoming titles

Autism and the Empathy Epidemic, Janet Harbold
Medical Humanities and Disability Studies, Stuart Murray
Reproductive Health, Literature, and Print Culture, 1650–1800, Ashleigh Blackwood

RELATING SUICIDE

A PERSONAL AND CRITICAL PERSPECTIVE

Anne Whitehead

BLOOMSBURY ACADEMIC
NEW YORK • LONDON • OXFORD • NEW DELHI • SYDNEY

BLOOMSBURY ACADEMIC
Bloomsbury Publishing Plc
50 Bedford Square, London, WC1B 3DP, UK
1385 Broadway, New York, NY 10018, USA
29 Earlsfort Terrace, Dublin 2, Ireland

BLOOMSBURY, BLOOMSBURY ACADEMIC and the Diana logo
are trademarks of Bloomsbury Publishing Plc

First published in Great Britain 2023

Cover design by Rebecca Heselton

A catalogue record for this book is available from the British Library.

A catalog record for this book is available from the Library of Congress.

ISBN: HB: 978-1-3501-9215-7
         PB: 978-1-3501-9216-4
         ePDF: 978-1-3501-9217-1
         eBook: 978-1-3501-9218-8

Series: Critical Interventions in the Medical and Health Humanities

Typeset by Integra Software Services Pvt. Ltd.
Printed and bound in Great Britain

To find out more about our authors and books visit www.bloomsbury.com
and sign up for our newsletters.

For my sister

'She is in the offing now.'

– Benjamin Myers, *The Offing*

CONTENTS

List of illustrations   x
Acknowledgements   xi

Introduction: Why?   1

1   When?   **15**
     A stopped watch   15
     The day in question   23
     In the nick of time   30

2   How?   **41**
     Drowning in cliché   41
     Pain scale   48
     Affective atmospheres   54

3   Where?   **69**
     A cracked barometer   69
     A wooden bench   78
     Communities of care   86

Coda: Who?   **97**

Bibliography   103
Index   109

ILLUSTRATIONS

1   The Stray, Redcar, August 2019. Photograph © the author   xii

2   My sister's watch, 2020. Photograph © the author   14

3   My sister, the Stray, Redcar, 1988. Photograph © the author   40

4   Tide clock, 2021. Photograph © the author   68

5   My sister, the Stray, Redcar, 1988. Photograph © the author   96

ACKNOWLEDGEMENTS

I offer my grateful thanks to the following:

Ben Doyle at Bloomsbury Academic for his unwavering support, from our original conversation through to publication.

Katrina Jaworski, Jeffrey Berman and the third, anonymous reader of the proposal for clarifying what I had already done and helping to see what might be possible.

Laura Cope and the series editors for their expert guidance throughout.

Newcastle University for granting me funded research leave, during which I was able to complete a full draft of the manuscript.

Paul Leworthy and Bàrbara Fernàndez Melleda of the Connecting Memories Network at Edinburgh University for their generous invitation to speak.

Linda Anderson, Kate Chedgzoy, Neil Gower, Alex Preston, Kimberley Reynolds and Margaret Wilkinson for giving valuable feedback on an early version.

Sinéad Morrissey, Kimberly Reynolds, Patricia Waugh, Angela Woods and Katrina Jaworski for their rigorous and careful attention to the full draft.

Bloodaxe Books for permission to quote from Joanne Limburg, *The Autistic Alice* (Bloodaxe Books, 2017) www.bloodaxebooks.com.

Picador Poetry for permission to quote from Denise Riley, *Say Something Back* © Denise Riley, 2016. Reproduced with permission of the Licensor through PLSclear.

Carcanet Press for permission to quote from 'The Way of Words and Language' by Elizabeth Jennings. From *The Collected Poems* (Carcanet Press), reproduced by permission of David Higham Associates.

Orlando von Einsiedel for permission to quote from *Evelyn* (Grain Media, 2018). The film is available to watch on Netflix.

Bloomsbury Press, for permission to quote from Benjamin Myers, *The Offing* © Benjamin Myers, 2019, reproduced courtesy of David Higham Associates.

Aileen Conlon, Kate Davies, Sarah Gott, Jane Grey, Catherine Johns, Rye Mattick and Neelam Srivastava for friendship and support along the way.

Dad, whose seat at the kitchen table is also empty now, and Mum, for sitting with me there remembering.

Figure 1 The Stray, Redcar, August 2019. Photograph © the author

INTRODUCTION
WHY?

A woman is on an early morning train, heading to a meeting. Her laptop is open on the table in front of her, and she is working through the emails in her inbox. She has just finished a cup of coffee that she grabbed on the station before boarding. Outside the window, fields blur past. Suddenly the train jerks, throwing everyone in the carriage a little forward or pressing them back against their seats, and comes to a standstill. There is a pause, but the train does not move forward. After five minutes, an announcement over the tannoy conveys that the train has collided with a person on the line. The atmosphere in the coach shifts and tenses – concern for the person who has died mingling with worries about how long the delay will be, and whether emails and texts of apology should yet be sent. The woman looks out at the fields, wondering who the family is and when they will be told the news. She tries not to think about what is happening on the track so that the train service can resume. She focuses, instead, on whether the driver of the train will have to be replaced and if this would be standard procedure when such an incident occurs.[1]

A second announcement advises that the delay to the service means that passengers can claim compensation on the price of their tickets. The train conductor gives the website address and advises that, in lieu of compensation, there will be an option to donate the money to the suicide charity, the Samaritans. The woman opens the website on her laptop, fills in the requested details and makes the donation. She emails her apologies for the meeting, explaining that she will join them as soon as she can. She continues to work through her inbox but is still aware of the bodily sensation of being jarred, thrown off balance, and it stays with her for the remainder of the day, lingering after she has left the train and after the meeting has concluded.

This book conceives of suicide as a jar or jolt in the texture of the everyday. I am concerned to ask how the encounter with suicide is felt, experienced and passed on. In the example I have just given, suicide is not only comprised of the train colliding with a person. It is registered as it disperses through an ever-widening network of people, agencies and actions – which include, but are not limited to, the driver stopping the train and reporting the incident, the train conductor making the announcement over the tannoy, the police being called to the scene and taking statements, passengers sending texts and emails, the Samaritans app that allows a donation to the charity to be made, and the relatives who still have to be told the news. Rather than seeing suicide as a solitary act, I am interested in tracing how it ripples out through a diverse range of bodies, institutions and objects, conceiving of suicide as relational in the ways that its dispersion connects lives which are otherwise unrelated.

My own encounter with suicide differs from the scenario I have just recounted. My sister walked into the sea when she was twenty-nine and I was twenty-seven. In relating suicide, then, I am also related to suicide; I have a familial kinship with it, and I am also connected to it through Donna Haraway's (2016) sense of kinship as a messy entanglement. My sister drowned between Redcar and Saltburn-by-the-Sea, on the north-east coast of England, on a stretch of beach known locally as the Stray. On 28 August 1998, my sister left the family home in Middlesbrough just after lunch, and her body was found on the beach that same evening. In the photograph of the Stray which precedes this Introduction (Figure 1), taken on another late August day two decades later, I am a little to the north of where my sister's body was found, at the place where she is most likely to have entered the water. The posts that lead into the sea in which she died have gaps between them, and this book does not attempt to fill in these spaces. I do not offer any explanation as to why my sister might have killed herself. The gap around which this book resonates honours my sister's own unstated reasons for ending her life on that day: she did not leave a suicide note behind. My focus lies, instead, on the processes that suicide's aftermath often involves: the rituals that help us to bridge a different gap, namely that between the extraordinary act of suicide and the everyday. In what follows, I examine how we live beside suicide in our quotidian lives and environments.

I have chosen not to relate here the story of why my sister's life matters. Judith Butler's concept of 'grievable life' (2004: 20) makes clear that grief is not a democracy: it privileges those who are most proximate to us. It aligns certain bodies and excludes others. My sister's life was, and is, both grievable and grieved. My concern is, rather, with how suicide comes to be materialized, which is also a question of how suicide comes to matter. I trace out the networks that surround the family's receipt of the news and which are common to how many deaths by suicide are experienced by relatives: the person (people) who find(s) the body, the police, the pathologist, the coroner, the funeral director. These various agencies are not incidental to suicide's materialization but integral to how suicide comes to be known – how, in other words, suicide is shaped, constructed, experienced, shared and related.

Angeliki Balayannis and Brian Robert Cook have observed that the production of knowledge on suicide 'severs self-destruction from time, space, and place' (2016: 530). While this abstraction of suicide facilitates 'the extension of knowledge across ever-larger epistemological scales', it also entails that 'the affective, emotional, and material aspects of self-destruction are rendered irrelevant, or at worst, made invisible' (2016: 530). Countering this tendency towards distance in suicide research, Balayannis and Cook argue for a 'partial, indirect, and relational' understanding of suicide, calling for a critical scholarship which is 'attentive to the materialities of suicide' (2016: 531). My approach converges with that of Balayannis and Cook, although my emphasis on the materialities of suicide emerges out of a personal experience of bereavement. Suicide is, for me, necessarily proximate, situated and embodied, and distanced objectivity perforce gives way to entangled relationality.

Therapist Alison Wertheimer has observed that suicide bereavement 'has traditionally been associated with a particularly difficult grief process compared to other losses' (2014: 23). The bereaved were seen to be vulnerable to severe grief, as well as to an increased risk of taking their own lives. This approach has recently been challenged by new research findings. Previous assumptions about suicide bereavement have been revised: Sheila E. Clark and Robert D. Goldney summarize, 'There are more similarities than differences in morbidity between those bereaved by suicide and through other causes, and the specific mode of death itself creates few if any quantitative differences in bereavement outcome after a suicide' (2000: 4–5). Wertheimer suggests that, in qualitative terms, suicide bereavement 'has certain things in common with … those bereaved as the result of a murder': death is 'sudden, untimely, and often violent' (2014: 151). Suicide bereavement also shares similarities with other deaths where those close to the deceased have not been present at the dying. These aspects of my sister's death produced in me an urgent need to know when, how and where her death had taken place. If we return to the scenario with which I began, the passengers on the train may question who has stepped into the path of the train, and why, but they have no cause to ask when, how or where because these are all embodied in the juddering moment when the train stopped.

Although my sister's drowning did not produce equivalent witnesses to her death, I was nevertheless able to arrive at a fuller picture of what happened with the help of those who attended her body in the following days. When, how and where are concerned with the material and relational aspects of suicide, locating the act in a grounded specificity.

The chapters of this book are structured around the sequence of events that often unfolds in the wake of a suicide, moving from the initial receipt of the news in Chapter 1, through the viewing and identification of the body, the post-mortem, and the inquest in Chapter 2, and closing with the ongoing grief process in Chapter 3. Unlike most critical approaches to suicide, I do not focus on what precedes or leads up to the suicidal act. This swivelling of attention to how suicide materializes in the wake of the death brings into view an alternative range of actors – rather than centring on mental health practitioners I am concerned with coronial law, building on Katrina Jaworski's groundbreaking work in this area. I situate the mortuary and the coroner's court as spaces in which suicide is made manifest in the everyday. Here, the meaning of suicide is constructed, contested and negotiated as the body of the deceased comes into contact with the bodies of medicine and of the law, and suicide is produced through an entanglement of the material and the discursive.

My approach to suicide has much in common with critical suicidology: I am interested in what the cultural, social, historical and political contexts of suicide contribute to our understanding. Jennifer White et al. have advocated for the inclusion of those with lived experience of suicidality in suicide research, pointing out that 'the voices of those who have "insider knowledge" have largely been erased in much of the published suicidology literature, which has tended to privilege the voices of researchers, academics, and other experts' (2016: 6–7). In addition to amplifying the need to listen to the voices of those who have survived a suicide attempt or intention, this book brings my personal experience of bereavement into the production of knowledge about suicide. While my encounter with suicide will inevitably differ from that of others whose relatives have ended their own lives, I hope some resonances remain and that any divergences in experience might lead to productive ongoing dialogue.

My work is distinct from critical suicidology in moving the focus away from suicide prevention. White et al. declare that their aim in *Critical Suicidology* is to 'invit[e] a fresh consideration of what suicide prevention work can and could involve' by 'creating a more expansive platform' (2016: 9) for hitherto marginalized voices. Ian Marsh, likewise, announces that the principal objective of *Suicide: Foucault, History and Truth* is to open up to scrutiny 'the assumptions embedded within accepted ways of thinking and practices with regard to suicide and suicide prevention in the clinical field' (2010: 7). I do not contest the importance of thinking critically about suicide prevention; a vital strand of work in this area connects suicide to questions of social justice (Button, 2016; Button and Marsh, 2019). Not every suicide *is* prevented, however, and this book accordingly centres on the question of suicide's aftermath. Here, too, I suggest, an approach that relates suicide out to broader institutional, social and political contexts is valuable, rather than focusing exclusively on an individualized (and often pathologized) grief process. Critical suicidology has arisen as a field in Australia and New Zealand, and my book adds to the momentum created by British scholars such as Amy Chandler, Ana Jordan and China Mills in relating its insights to the UK context. In particular, I consider Jaworski's work on the Australian coronial system in the light of changes in English coronial law over the two decades since my sister's death.

This book continues my work in the critical medical humanities, bringing it into dialogue with critical suicidology. Angela Woods and I argued of the 'primal scene' of the medical humanities, namely the clinical encounter between practitioner and patient in which the unfolding of the cancer diagnosis takes place:

> We need to open up possibilities for the medical humanities to operate in radically different arenas of critical consideration. … How might the bodies of doctors and patients be marked in terms of race, class, gender, ability and disability, and with what effects? What else … is in the room, and with what forms or modes of agency might it be associated? How might we account for non-human objects and presences, for belief systems, and even for the diagnosis itself – what, for example, is its history, or its status as a performative act? Where and when else might the scene be situated, and what difference would this make?
>
> (2016: 2)

This study opens up to analysis the spaces associated with the coronial process: the mortuary and the coroner's court. I focus on how the body of the deceased is marked by gender, in ways that can affect the coronial outcome or verdict. I take into account a variety of non-human objects in the course of this study; in relation to my sister's death, I pay close attention to her watch, which accrues its own agency and vitality.[2] I think about suicide as verdict and about how it is performatively named (or not) at the close of an inquest hearing. I trace the legal history of suicide as a criminal act and the lingering effects of this status in the contemporary coroner's court. My study also takes entanglement, which is a key organizing principle of the critical medical humanities, as central to its methodology. I argue that the materialization of suicide is enacted through the coming together of multiple objects, people, practices and discourses. Suicide, in other words, is not only a pre-existing, material act. It is also constituted after the fact through the coronial process or network, which comprises the autopsy and the inquest. This critical focus on entanglement requires us to examine how knowledge works and with what effects. It also entails that suicide is a local, rather than a universal, phenomenon.

The critical medical humanities has been centrally preoccupied with the narrative articulation of illness and pathology. The first wave of the medical humanities was animated by the rise of pathography as a literary genre and its notable success within the publishing marketplace. Arthur Frank influentially argued that, if illness disturbs or disrupts an individual's ability to make meaning and to order experience, narrative can help to restore this function; in his terms, the 'chaos narrative' that is 'sucked into the undertow of illness and the disasters that attend it' can give way to the 'quest narrative', in which illness becomes a resource through which the individual is transformed into someone new (1995: 115). Angela Woods has persuasively contested Frank's privileging of a certain form of narrative – realist, linear and teleological – over other, more contingent and fragmentary modes, as well as querying the 'monopoly on expressivity' that Frank accords to narrative itself, and she urges us to look to other forms of expression (2012: 126). The critical medical humanities has also witnessed a turn to chronic rather than acute experiences of illness, which further pressure Frank's model of narrative (as) reorientation or recovery.

Andrew Bennett has aptly noted that the narrative problem with suicide is that it 'offer[s] teleological and hermeneutic *form* to the chance and contingency of a life' (2017: 178). Once suicide marks its ending, he observes, '*Everything* in the narrative of an individual life can be seen to be accounted for (or at least can be subject to) the *telos* of a suicide' (2017: 178). Teleology does not here lead to the restitution of meaning, as it does for Frank. Rather, Bennett remarks that the suicide memoir, a genre which emerged in the late twentieth century, repeatedly rehearses the impossibility of making meaning out of a death by suicide. Bennett observes that the genre 'has a particular *topos* ... that is different from other kinds of elegy and memoir because of its focus on the central unanswerable and irresolvable question of *why* the death occurred' (2017: 181). For Bennett, writers of suicide memoirs are caught in an unending cycle of repetition-compulsion, in which 'the mourning work of writing works through the traumatic and intractable conundrum (the traumatically intractable conundrum) of another's suicide' (2017: 181–2). My study accords more agency and creativity to the bereaved by turning the volume down on that insistent why (and on the insistence that why must be the central question). Thinking with and through a range of suicide texts, I examine their relation of suicide as a part of everyday life. I include suicide memoirs and novels among the texts that I discuss, but I also turn to poetry, documentary film and vernacular memorials, as alternative forms of meaning-making in the wake of suicide.

There are surprisingly few critical studies of suicide in literature, given the prevalence of its representation in the modern and contemporary canon. Jeffrey Berman's *Surviving Literary Suicide* shares the preoccupations of first-wave medical humanities, in its concern with whether the expression of suicidal ideation in literature can shift the writer's attitude towards the act itself and function as a support system. Berman opens his study by asking: 'Can literature play a role in suicide prevention?' (1999: 1). He responds by arguing that literature is a necessary, but at times insufficient, vehicle for relieving suicidal intentionality, reading across four writers who wrote about suicide and then ended their lives (Virginia Woolf, Ernest Hemingway, Sylvia Plath and Anne Sexton) and two writers who, in his terms, survived their own act of literary suicide (Kate Chopin and William Styron). Berman grounds his study in pedagogy, through which he examines the impact of suicide literature on the reader, considering his students' affective responses as recorded in class diaries. This aspect of his writing connects to wider cultural anxieties that the representation of suicide might act as a form of contagion, and Berman ponders whether reading a literary suicide text might potentially 'endanger a reader's health', concluding that 'there is some evidence to suggest that the glorification of suicide may endanger certain people' (1999: 3).

Andrew Bennett's *Suicide Century* counters Berman's emphasis on identification, even to the point of mimicry, opining that novels of suicidal ideation 'remind us that what the literary novel more generally is *for* involves not so much a ... refined form of empathy as an appreciation of empathy's limits' (2017: 24). Bennett positions suicide literature as 'ambiguously curative', drawing on the *pharmakon* as at once both poison and cure,

7

such that it 'offers a space in which suicide can be thought, where it can be imagined, even when it cannot be imagined elsewhere' (2017: 11). Of most relevance to my concerns, Bennett contends that the turn of the twentieth century witnessed the emergence in literature 'of the act [of suicide] ... as everyday, or quotidian': in the works of the key modernist writers, suicide became 'pervasive', 'normalized' and 'unremarkable' (2017: 23). Although my focus is on contemporary texts, Chapter 1 examines Virginia Woolf's modernist treatment of suicide in *Mrs. Dalloway* ([1925] 2000). I also expand on Bennett by locating in Charles Dickens's *Bleak House* ([1852–3] 2008) a nineteenth-century precursor to modernism's absorption of suicide into the commonplace. Throughout, I ask how a range of writers have stitched suicide into the fabric of the everyday. More than this, suicide reveals, in the eloquent words of Laura Salisbury, that 'the extraordinary [is] a quality furled inside the very fabric of the common', and suicide accordingly registers in the texts I discuss as something that is 'always and everywhere immanent' in our quotidian environments (2016: 458).[3]

I situate my critical approach at the intersection of feminist theory and the affective turn, looking to an influential strand of work that has, as Carolyn Pedwell and I have summarized, '[brought] serious attention (back) to the substance and significance of matter, materiality and the body' (2012: 117). My understanding of suicide as an unanticipated jolt or judder speaks to Kathleen Stewart's formulation of ordinary affect, which is structured around jarring encounters that disrupt the everyday and, in so doing, connect people together to create the common experiences that shape public feeling. For Elizabeth Grosz, too, being jarred out of our immersion in time can be generative in helping us to grasp transformative potential, and I draw on her concept of the 'nic[k]' of time (2004: 5) to ask what alternative possibilities for living might be opened up by the encounter with suicide. Other feminist critics have been more cautious about the potential for change associated with the force of affect: Sara Ahmed has noted that affects often attach us to social norms and (re)produce existing hierarchies and exclusions. Ahmed accordingly insists on the intertwining of the affective and the structural, which recognizes and accounts for the ways in which 'feelings might be how structures get under our skin' (2010: 216). I draw on Ahmed's concept of 'sticky' objects (2004: 11) to ask how our attachment to things can expose and illuminate sites of personal and social tension, attending in particular to the structures of family and the law. Ann Cvetkovich, too, is wary of any easy or straightforward equation between a shift in affect and meaningful social or political change. She nevertheless foregrounds the ways in which a focus on public feelings might move feminist theory beyond critique and exposure. Her work underpins my consideration of vernacular memorials in Chapter 3, helping me to identify affective materialities that can offer an alternative to clinical models of grief and that afford performative vocabularies of community and of hope.

My privileging of the material and relational aspects of suicide necessitates that my discussion is grounded in specific localities. In itself, this represents a significant contribution to critical approaches to suicide, which have tended to privilege space, understood as an objectively defined area, over place, which is imbued with meaning through everyday social practices. Suicide is mapped onto geographical areas in disciplines such as health population studies and sociology, but there has been less attention to how we live beside suicide in our daily habits and routines. The places of suicide I discuss centre on the British context. In Chapter 1, I open out from the place of my sister's death to the River Ouse in Sussex where Virginia Woolf drowned, emphasizing that both locations comprise ordinary, working environments. Chapter 3 begins with another river – the River Foyle that runs through Derry-Londonderry – which has become a public place of suicide in the years following the Troubles. I move to Peterborough Railway Station as the quotidian setting for the suicide that opens Louise Doughty's *Platform Seven* (2019), before closing with the various rural locations in *Evelyn* (2018) – the Cairngorms, the Lake District, the South Downs – where the von Einsiedel siblings walk to remember their brother's death. Suicide, I suggest, unsettles our relation to place, especially if it happens in a public location. A beach, a railway platform or a bridge represents at once an everyday, if not banal, setting and a highly cathected memorial site, and it can be difficult to navigate between the two realities. My interest in how suicide is related in and through community networks chimes with recent anthropological and ethnographic approaches to suicide. I am indebted to Lisa Stevenson's (2014) ethnography of suicide in Iqaluit, the capital of Canada's north-easternmost territory, and Jocelyn Lim Chua's (2014) ethnography of the southern Indian state of Kerala, the nation's suicide capital. In both studies, place is layered, dynamic and shifting, and I share their interest in capturing the multiple, embodied and messy interactions between suicide and place.

Chapter 1 addresses the question of when, focusing on suicide's materialization in time. My sister's watch threads through the chapter, and I follow its movement in the immediate aftermath of her death, as the watch became the first means of identifying her body. Thinking of the watch in terms of Ahmed's 'sticky' object (2004: 11), I ask how the feelings with which it is invested open out to broader structural concerns, and I pair the watch with the alarm clock that keeps time in Lisa Stevenson's study of suicide among the Inuit youth, an object which is also sticky in its associations. We tend to describe the time of suicide in terms of the date, rather than the day, on which it occurred, and I move on to consider what we might gain by relating suicide to the temporal framework of the day. Building on Bennett's observation that modernist literature marked the advent of suicide as quotidian, I read Woolf's *Mrs. Dalloway* as an experiment in stitching suicide into the fabric of an unremarkable Wednesday in June. I close by turning to Grosz's nick in time as a framework for the suicidal journey. Once a certain tipping point in suicidal ideation has been reached, we often think of suicide as fixed and unalterable in its course, preventable only through the intervention of an external party. Drawing on Olivia Stevenson, I indicate that we might accord more agency and adaptability to the suicidal, as well as listen carefully to those who have survived a suicide attempt and/or intention. The teleology of suicide – its drive towards the end – is at stake here, and I hold open a space in which we might (re)conceive the suicidal act in terms of the uncertain present of its unfolding. I read Olivia Laing's memoir *To the River* (2012) as indicative of the challenges of resisting suicide's teleological imperative, yet to fail to do so can, I argue, have consequences for how suicide materializes.

Chapter 2 centres on the question of how. I begin by addressing Yiyun Li's description of the immediate aftermath of a suicide as 'cliché-land' (2019: 9), asking how cliché operates in this context. Drawing on Denise Riley, I position cliché as a linguistic mode that represents a common idiom, and I suggest that it can act as an important resource in the wake of suicide. The second section considers the viewing of the body and the autopsy. Kay Redfield Jamison has described the family's identification of the body at the morgue as 'unimaginable' (1999: 66). I contend that it is vital to engage with the space of the mortuary. Building on Jaworski, I examine the role of the post-mortem in establishing suicidal intentionality. I highlight the tension that commonly exists for relatives between the knowledge the autopsy can bring and the damage it inflicts on the body. The chapter's closing section turns to the inquest. I argue that Dickens's depiction of coronial law in *Bleak House* connects suicide not to individual intention but to social and environmental harms, articulating a new, atmospheric mode of relating suicide. I conclude by surveying the contemporary inquest, focusing on the retaining of the criminal standard of evidence in suicide cases in England

and Wales after the decriminalization of suicide in 1961. My attention to the question of evidence, and its entanglement with the production of objects of knowledge, picks up a key theme of the critical medical humanities (Whitehead and Woods, 2016: 15) and uses it to reflect on the intersection between medical and legal procedure.

Chapter 3 turns to the question of where. I open with the geographical mapping of suicide onto region, which has revealed in the UK a marked correlation between suicide and socio-economic deprivation. I compare two memoirs of growing up in Derry-Londonderry – Darran Anderson's *Inventory* (2020) and Kerri ní Dochartaigh's *Thin Places* (2021) – to ascertain how contemporary writers have related suicide's connection to a place that has been politically divided and economically left behind. My analysis overlaps with social justice approaches to suicide, which move beyond a sociological mapping of incidences of suicide to advocate for structural reform and economic investment. My approach nevertheless differs from social justice approaches in its understanding of how change works; following Carolyn Pedwell (2021), I consider the transformation of minor habits to be as meaningful as major revolutions, and the chapter's second section accordingly examines the potential of everyday practices of vernacular memorialization in the context of suicide. I discuss my own negotiation of the place where my sister died, by visiting Antony Gormley's sculpture *Another Place*, installed near Liverpool in 2005, in which the cast-iron figures on the beach are continuously submerged and revealed by the ebb and flow of the tide. The chapter ends by considering grief as a continuing bond, which chimes with the recent shift in the critical medical humanities from acute to chronic temporalities. I read the enactment of care in von Einsiedel's documentary *Evelyn*, in which the siblings' compassion for one another expands out to friends, strangers and the audience, as a means of generating community and solidarity around suicide by harnessing the potential of the local and the relational.

The coda to this book takes up the question of who, which has threaded through the preceding chapters. Who, I ask, is marginalized in the current configurations through which suicide is materialized? How might these configurations potentially change to become more inclusive and diverse? Throughout this book, I relate the act of suicide out to its contexts of time, place and other people. I close by situating this work of relating as ongoing, offering up ideas raised in the chapters to the future contexts of wider medical, legal and societal change.

Positioned in suicide's aftermath, my book is aligned with what Christina Sharpe has designated as 'wake work' (2016: 17). Gathering the different resonances of what it means to be 'in the wake', Sharpe writes:

> Wakes are processes; through them we think about the dead and our relations to them; they are rituals through which to enact grief and memory. Wakes allow those among the living to mourn the passing of the dead through ritual; they are the watching of relatives and friends beside the body of the deceased from death to burial and the accompanying drinking, feasting, and other observances. ... But wakes are also the tracks left on the water's surface ... ; the disturbance caused by a body swimming, or one that is moved, in water; ... a region of disturbed flow; ... finally, wake means being awake and, also, consciousness.
>
> (2016: 21)

Sharpe enacts a movement of expansion out from the dead, and the observances of mourning, to wider connections and associations.[4] This book, too, begins with the body of the deceased, and broadens out from there, in temporal, spatial and conceptual terms. Writing in the wake of suicide entails thinking about the processes and rituals, public and private, through which we both make sense of and give meaning to death. Living in the wake of my sister's suicide means living in the disturbance caused by her body's movement through the water, and I have found the reality of her drowning painful, and at times overwhelming, to confront. Nevertheless, a region of disturbed flow causes things to surface, it can unsettle productively as well as negatively, and I ask in the following pages whether situating ourselves in the wake of suicide might animate potentially transformative questions about the ways in which we relate to others and the possibilities of relating (to) suicide otherwise.

Notes

1   The replacement of the train driver in the event of a fatality on the line is standard practice, as outlined on the Network Rail website: 'The driver of the train will be relieved of their duties (to allow the process of counselling to begin) and be replaced' ('Fatalities').

2   This book's focus on suicide's aftermath entails that I am principally concerned with the agency of objects in relation to those left behind. Katrina Jaworski has considered the agency of objects in the suicidal act, noting the entanglement of material objects, such as guns and pills, and methods of suicide (2015: 187–8). Jaworski also notes that the agency of objects, as theorised by Bruno Latour, complicates the attribution of action and agency to the human as a sovereign source of intention in suicide. Seeing objects as agential, Jaworski observes, involves the recognition that intentions are affected by objects, which necessarily shape 'the particularities of suicide as performance' (2015: 190).

3   Salisbury writes with reference to Virginia Woolf's essay 'On Being Ill' ([1930] 2012), noting that, in Woolf, 'illness is both the instigator of revelation and the ordinary run of things' (2016: 458). Although Woolf's essay is primarily concerned with physical illness – the headache and influenza – her writing also encompasses mental illness, which, according to Salisbury, 'remains at the core of Woolf's radical modernist proposition' (2016: 457).

4   For Sharpe, living in the wake refers to occupying 'the continuous and changing present of slavery's as yet unresolved unfolding' (2016: 14) and her vocabulary of drowning takes on particular political charge in this context.

Figure 2 My sister's watch, 2020. Photograph © the author

1
WHEN?

A stopped watch

I begin with a watch. It was my sister's watch. It lies on the desk beside me as I type these words: a thoroughly unremarkable object.

It has taken me twenty years to bring this object into my house. I have known exactly where the watch was: in a box that was kept in the sideboard of my parents' home. At any time, I could have taken the box out of the sideboard and the watch out of the box. But I had not needed, or desired, to have the watch to hand until last year. Then the desire or the need – I am not sure how best to describe the insistent urge I then experienced – to have the watch by my side led me to open the sideboard and to take out the box.

I open this chapter by asking what it means to live beside suicide. The watch gives me one way of responding to this question. The watch was kept in a sideboard, in a box. I was reassured by knowing that it was there, but I did not open the box or take the watch out. Twenty years had passed after my sister's death before I felt ready to look at the watch again, an object I had last seen on her wrist when she was alive. Living beside suicide is a matter of time. It is also about how time itself comes to matter.

I now keep the watch on a shelf in the bureau of my study. It has found its place beside my stapler, a tin of paperclips and a bottle of ink. I have filed the watch with the odds and ends of my writing life: within reach of my desk, but not, like my laptop, pens, pencils and notepaper, on the desk. I handle the watch as I do the bottle of ink, putting it on the desk when it has work to do or, more exactly, when the work of writing cannot be done without it. The watch feels as integral to the composition of this book as the ink which forms the words that you are currently reading.

Some objects, like ink on a printed page, create an impression; they impress themselves upon us. Sara Ahmed has written of the ways in which an object of feeling, an object like my sister's watch, 'both shapes and is shaped by emotions' (2004: 8). The object impresses upon us; it leaves its mark or trace because it has already been in contact with other people and objects, and it has become suffused with their histories. For Ahmed, such an object, gathering these histories of contact, becomes 'sticky, or saturated with affect' (2004: 11). It generates an emotional response: we are drawn toward, or propelled away from, an object of this kind. It may be unremarkable enough, but it is not neutral. It provokes feeling.

The watch is, by definition, an intimate object. It is worn next to the skin. There is a discernible crease in the leather strap of my sister's watch on the hole nearest to its face. If I put the watch onto my own wrist, I use the same hole to secure it in place. Its casing rubs against my skin and, when I take the watch off, I can see the faint mark of where it has been. The rubbing of the watch carries the history of its contact with my sister and generates not only a physical trace but also an affective intensity, which I struggle to name as a particular emotion. It is, nevertheless, as tangible as the fine film of sweat which forms where the watch has been in contact with my skin. It is the frisson of an ongoing connection.

Ahmed has observed of the sticky object: 'The object may stand in for other objects or may be proximate to other objects' (2004: 8). The watch binds us together because of its proximate relation; it creates the same impression on my skin that it left on my sister's. The watch can also stand in for my sister, in a metonymic relation to her, and it is this mode of relation that propels me away from it. In this capacity, the watch becomes too proximate – not to my sister, but to the event of her death. This contiguity means that, even now, I live beside the watch by handling it as an object connected to my writing practice.

Let's take a closer look at the watch (Figure 2) and record some details. Its face is scratched in places, showing more wear than the strap, which suggests that the latter was replaced not long before my sister died. The watch has stopped at twenty-three minutes past six. If I turn it over, the back of its case is inscribed with the words: 'Water Resistant Plastics'.

My sister was wearing this watch on the day she died. It is the only material witness that I have. The watch entered the sea with my sister, and it came out with her, too, still on her wrist when her body was found. What does the watch then become? A witness? A relic? A substitute, at any rate, which enables me to speak of my sister's death. The stopped watch becomes a proxy for the death of my sister. It is an object that you and I can both look at and consider. We can pick it up, turn it over and put it back down again.

If the watch stands in for my sister, offering me a way of looking at her death and of showing it to you, then the symbolism it holds is not straightforward. To stand as a proxy for my sister's death, or as a witness to it, the watch would have stopped as her life ended. The seawater would have flooded its mechanism, as it saturated my sister's lungs, and the hands of the watch, forever stuck at twenty-three minutes past six, would commemorate the moment that both she and it succumbed. This was not what happened. The plastic of the watch's casing was water-resistant, and the watch was still going when it came out of the sea. The time it now displays represents the moment when its battery ran flat, as it lay in its box in the sideboard. The watch provokes in me a feeling of irritation, which derives from a sense that it betrayed my sister in carrying on when she did not. As a keeper of time, it failed to record the moment that my sister's life stopped, even though it succeeded brilliantly on its own stated terms of keeping going when submerged in water.

Although the watch acts as an imperfect witness to my sister's death, its subsequent movements trace the immediate impact of her suicide on the family. The police removed the watch from my sister's wrist so that it could be used as a means of identification, prior to the formal identification of her body at the mortuary. At the family home, the police asked my parents a series of routine questions to ascertain whether the body washed up on the beach was my sister's. The process stumbled momentarily as my parents were asked whether she wore any jewellery. They replied in the negative, thinking of the rings, necklaces and earrings which my sister did not wear. It was, surely, somebody else's daughter that had been found. But a watch also counts as jewellery, and the answer was yes after all. The watch was produced and claimed by my parents, as my sister's body would be a few hours later. Part of the watch's stickiness lies in its transformation into an object that was bagged and labelled as an item of evidence in a case. This, too, leaves an affective residue behind.

Katrina Jaworski and Daniel G. Scott have described the moment when the news of suicide is received by the family as a complicated tangle of 'shock, disbelief, and numbness', asking: 'What happens in those moments when incomprehension sets in, when silence begins to mark the intelligibility of suicide?' (2016: 209). Responding to this question, Jaworski and Scott turn to the matter of time. Suicide, they suggest, manifests as a disturbance or disruption of time:

> [S]uicide can be interpreted as a rupture, not because it *is* suicide, but because it becomes a tear in the time of one's life. To draw on a metaphor, imagine that life is like a piece of fabric. And suddenly, for

no reason at all, there is a sudden rip that yanks at the fabric. It tears the surface and marks it forever even if someone mends it later on.

(2016: 214)

The piece of fabric is an object – like the watch – marked by its contact with suicide. It will always bear the trace of that contact. For Jaworski and Scott, the shock of suicide is experienced as a thickening of, or density in, our everyday sense of time: 'the suddenness of the news, the dead body in the room, the police late at night, and the insistence it must be a mistake all mark a texture of time' (2016: 215). We are jarred out of our habitual perception of time as ongoing, sequential and causal in the sense that one moment flows inevitably into the next. Time slows and becomes viscous, and movement through it feels exhausting.

I heard the news of my sister's death the following morning. I was immediately propelled into a different experience of time. For some days, I was confused about the day on which my sister had died, unable to comprehend that she had left the family home just after lunch and that her body had been found washed onto the beach in the evening of that same day. I had been told that we did not know the time of my sister's death, only that it had taken place sometime between mid-afternoon and early evening. Even so, and without any sense of contradiction, I was convinced that my sister's watch had stopped in the water. This belief reflects the state designated by Denise Riley as 'arrested time' ([2012] 2019: 13), which made the watch's onward movement a matter of complete implausibility. Even now, when I look at the watch's face, I see two distinct and irreconcilable temporalities: time continuing and time abruptly stopped. Neither of these temporalities cancels out the other. They co-exist as different ways of experiencing what it means to inhabit time.

Riley has described this distinctive doubling or splitting of time in relation to receiving the unexpected news of her son's death from an undiagnosed heart condition.[1] She writes: 'the experience that not only preoccupied but occupied me was of living in suddenly arrested time: that acute sensation of being cut off from any temporal flow' ([2012] 2019: 13). Following my sister's death, I, too, occupied a time stripped of chronology. I marked time but there was no corresponding sense of progression. I recall noting down for myself: I must remember this once I have returned to the press and the urgency of things. I must retain something of this other time. Riley resists the language of trauma or pathology, speaking of a state that is 'not uncommon' ([2012] 2019: 15) and that has 'a half-tellable ordinariness' to it ([2012] 2019: 19). The different texture of time, exposed through a sudden death, reveals our experience of time to be mutable rather than fixed.

The difficulty in inhabiting this static temporal state is not, Riley notes, inherent in the experience itself but rather in its communication: 'Hard to put into words, yet absolutely lucid as you inhabit it daily, this sensation of having been lifted clean out of habitual time only becomes a trial if you try to make it intelligible to others who've not experienced it' ([2012] 2019: 15–16). Although the state is shared by many, it is not often represented. For Riley, the issue becomes one not of language but of form. Form is the vessel in which our words are held, the container that gives them shape and definition. Narrative, with its forward progression and its propulsion towards an ending, is attuned to our habitual sense of chronological time. Although it can subvert this tendency, narrative often falters in the face of an arrested or paralysed temporality. This does not mean that we should give up on representation altogether.[2] Katrina Jaworski has observed that 'poetry's form … offers a different kind of structure and space for saying things about suicide that might otherwise be too difficult to say' (2020a: 166). For Riley, poetry can capture what it means to live atemporally. She distinguishes poetry from narrative in terms of its temporal movement: 'A poem may well be carried by oscillation, a to-and-fro, rather than by some forward-leaning chronological drive. It both sanctions and enacts an experience of time that is not linear' ([2012] 2019: 76). Rhyme is repetition with difference, and, returning to the image of a torn piece of fabric, Riley indicates that it can begin the work of 'making a chain of varied sound-stitches across time, a link to represent that feeling of sequence which may have been lost' ([2012] 2019: 77). Poetry is not a cure – it cannot 'mend the split' in the fabric ([2012] 2019: 77) – but neither is it reflective of stasis. It can 'unobtrusively, hesitantly – even reluctantly – fin[d] a first breath of [stopped time's] future' ([2012] 2019: 78).[3]

In the weeks following my sister's death I carried Elizabeth Jennings's poem, 'The Way of Words and Language', like a talisman. I had come across it when I was looking for readings for my sister's funeral, and, although it was not read at the service, I associate the poem closely with this time. When I first read the poem, occupied with having a body to bury, I interpreted its 'you' as my sister. Lost 'near home', and with 'your watch … stopped', she had become a 'sea ghost' (2012: 538). The poem comforted me with its assurance that 'you / Are found and safe at last' (2012: 539). The sea had washed my sister's body back onto the beach, and we were able to lay her to rest. Reading the poem again recently, I saw the 'you' as my younger self, suspended without my usual bearings and 'see[ing] in the mirror a ghost' (2012: 538). The poem navigates between the 'time of silence' (539) and the forward progression of the morning light rising over the coast, without ultimately reconciling the two. But perhaps the hold that the poem had on me was related more to the 'minute work' ([2012] 2019: 77) of rhyme and rhythm, to which Riley refers. Jennings has crafted a complex series of echoes and resonances, oscillating between rhymes and half-rhymes, and she revolves her words – 'lost', 'ghost', 'time', 'night', 'light' (2012: 538–9) – as tenderly and carefully as the sea caresses the 'pale, rubbed pebble' (2012: 538) in the slowly turning tide.

Rhythm, intensity, resonance: if poetry can convey the texture of arrested time, then it is not directly but through a performative invocation. We are no longer in control of time, planning our schedule according to the regular segments of minutes and hours on the watch's face. Rather, we succumb to time's unpredictable rhythms and forces as they play through and across the poem. Elizabeth Grosz has described the surprising, mobile force of time as a 'nick' or a 'cut', which we do not apprehend epistemologically – as in reading a watch's face – but rather catch in glimpses out of the corner of our eye:

Time is neither fully 'present', a thing in itself, nor is it a pure abstraction. … It cannot be viewed directly, nor can it be eliminated from pragmatic consideration. It is a kind of evanescence that appears only at those moments when our expectations are (positively or negatively) surprised. We can think it only when we are jarred out of our immersion in its continuity, when something untimely disrupts our expectations. … We can think it only in passing moments, through ruptures, nicks, cuts, in instances of dislocation … events that disrupt our immersion in and provoke our conceptualization of temporal continuity.

(2004: 5)

Suicide, and other sudden forms of bereavement, comprise those jarring moments; nicks or cuts in the fabric of time that not only dislocate us from the flow of time but that also, and in so doing, reveal the very experience of temporal continuity to have been a construct all along. It becomes apparent, from this new vantage point, that time is not singular, after all, and that we routinely inhabit multiple temporalities.

A second object to place beside the watch: an alarm clock. It is the old-fashioned type of clock with a large round face and a bell on top. It sits by the bed in a black-and-white photograph of an Inuit tent, and a mother sits on the bed holding her baby. The photograph was taken in Lake Harbour in July 1955, and it appeared in a Canadian government publication. It was reproduced in Lisa Stevenson's study of the suicide epidemic among the Canadian Inuit, which has extended from the 1980s to the present. The photograph is striking because there are, in fact, not one but two alarm clocks sitting side by side next to the bed. There is something eerie, if not uncanny, in their doubled effect, which was picked up in the original caption to the photograph that posed the question: 'Why two clocks?' (2014: 141).

Stevenson notes that the image of two alarm clocks repeats itself across the archival record. In her account, the clock is a decidedly sticky object: its presence in an Inuit dwelling was a manifestation of the regulated life that the Canadian colonial administration was trying to impose, disciplining an Inuit family to rise at the same time each day, regardless of the season, and to attend work or school. The clock declares that time is singular; we consult it so that we can ascertain what the correct time is. The presence of two clocks, ticking side by side, is a jarring moment – one of Grosz's nicks or cuts – because it disrupts our immersion in time, rendering it visible to us. Stevenson aptly observes: 'So we have the doubling of something that usually exists by itself (one clock at the side of a bed, as a token of the category clock, as a token of time passing) here appearing in a pair, disrupting our sense that we *know* what a clock is for, that we *know* what a clock, or time, is' (2014: 144).

If the single clock represents the attempted transformation of the Inuit into 'successful bureaucratic subjects' (2014: 146), two clocks are suggestive of a relation to time that does not accord with this regulated life. Stevenson's anthropological work with the Inuit uncovers a proliferation of alternative ways of being in time, which prompts her to question the relation between suicide and time: 'At what cost do Inuit youth belong, as they do, to Canadian bureaucratic society? … With what words do we describe the pain of *also* belonging to another time – that of the unfound Eskimos [sic], that of driving around and around, or that of the dream world? How do we pose the question of suicide alongside the question of time?' (2014: 147). Stevenson raises an important concern that has threaded through this section. What does it mean if suicide inhabits one temporality – time without flow, the time of two clocks – but if it is primarily understood in relation to another (bureaucratic time)? 'The clock', Stevenson concludes, 'has no time for suicide, … and so it ticks inexorably on' (2014: 147).

I have placed the alarm clock beside the watch to suggest a resonance between these two objects. They are not the same, and the differences between them matter because they speak to the ways in which suicide is a temporal – as in, an historical – act. The alarm clock circulates within a colonial regime, as a means of reshaping the Inuit world through the repetition of new habits and norms. The two clocks are difficult to read as a response, poised between affective investment and insubordination. Their presence side by side in the room creates a feeling; it represents what Ahmed has described as 'a thickness in the air, or an atmosphere' (2004: 10). The twinned clocks draw our attention, and, in so doing, they create tension. My sister's watch circulates within the familial space, and it connects my body to hers, as well as to the family home. The watch was also a point of contact with the institution of the law, which has left its own residue. It is a reminder that, in suicide, the personal and the public take shape in and through each other. This contact with the law marked the watch as part of a case, which was shaped by English coronial procedure of the late twentieth century.

The watch and the clock are, nevertheless, intimately connected as time pieces. They are functional objects, which form a habitual part of our everyday lives. Merging the alarm clock with the watch, Stevenson observes:

> We wear clocks, as watches, on our bodies like a second skin. It becomes hard to say whether the clock becomes like us, with its 'hands' and its 'face', or we become like the clock, experiencing our bodies as biological clocks. What is certain is that the clock becomes such a familiar tool that we can only represent it to ourselves, only truly notice its presence in a moment of shock.
>
> (2014: 142)

Suicide and other untimely deaths constitute defamiliarizing moments of shock, which render the clock, and the experience of time itself, present to us. In telling the story of what it means to live beside suicide through the mundane objects of a watch and an alarm clock, I have indicated that its impact is registered in the material stuff of the everyday. My feelings about my sister's suicide are generated, in part, in and through my contact with her watch. In this sense, suicide is legible in terms of what Kathleen Stewart has designated ordinary affect: 'Ordinary affect is a surging, a rubbing, a connection of some kind that has an impact. It's ... not about one person's feelings becoming another's but about bodies literally affecting one another and generating intensities' (2007: 128). Ordinary affect is experienced as the contact of one surface against another: it describes the friction or the fraying that is produced. My sister's watch rubs against my skin, connecting me back to my sister, and it also rubs me up the wrong way. The watch is what Stewart designates as a 'moving thin[g]' (2007: 4), both in its 'capacity to affect and to be affected' (2007: 4), and in its literal motion, which maps out connections, routes and circuits: between people, between objects and between institutions. Taking its cue from Stewart, this section has accordingly directed its descriptive effort not towards finally 'know[ing]' the watch, but towards 'performing some of the intensity and texture that makes [it] habitable and animate' (2007: 4).

The day in question

> On 13 October 1991, my grandparents killed themselves. It was a Sunday. Not really the ideal day of the week for suicide. On Sundays, family members call each other and friends drop in to go walking the dogs with you. I'd have thought a Monday, for instance, much more suitable. But there we are; it was a Sunday; it was in October. I picture a clear autumn day because it all happened in Denmark.
>
> (Adorján, [2009] 2012: 1)

This passage, which forms the striking opening to Johanna Adorján's memoir of her grandparents, exposes an incongruity between suicide and a day of the week. Sunday is deemed inappropriate for suicide, but is Monday any more suitable, despite the narrator's protestations? When I speak of my sister's death, the date serves as a commemorative marker, but there is something jarring in saying that my sister killed herself on a Friday. The two terms, the suicide and the day, as opposed to the date, on which it happened rub against one another. How might we account for this friction? What makes a Friday or a Sunday – or a Monday or a Tuesday – incommensurate with the suicidal act?[4]

Adorján goes on to reconstruct imaginatively her grandparents' last day. She asks: 'What do people do on the morning that they know will be their last? I imagine that they tidy up, get things done. Take out the rubbish, file away last month's telephone bill, fold clean underclothes and make sure to smooth out those already folded before putting them away – after all, they will be seen by the eyes of others' ([2009] 2012: 20). Adorján focuses on the routines and actions of the ordinary day, tasks repeated so often that we typically perform them in a distracted or involuntary manner. In her description, there seems to be a newly self-conscious aspect to these mundane habits. They are undertaken in the knowledge that their results will soon be on public display. Perhaps they are a means of preparing for what is to come: a final putting in order. I do not need to imagine what my sister did on her last morning. I know her time was spent in an equivalent manner: washing, dressing, tidying, folding and sorting. Everything was neatly put away. How do we put the ordinary morning next to the suicide later in the day? What does it mean to think the two together in the framework of a single day?

My sister died on a late August Friday, leading into the Bank Holiday weekend. I was staying with friends, and we visited a local National Trust property. I had taken my camera and, when I finally got round to developing the roll of film over a year later, each photograph was stamped on the reverse with the date and time the image had been taken. And so, I know that at 13.02 I was examining the medieval timbering of the house. At 15.23, I was looking up at a swallow's nest among the wooden beams of the entrance gate. At 17.46, I was in a pub garden, gazing at the summer sky. How do I put these moments beside my sister's death? There is synchronicity here, although my knowledge of my sister's movements on that day is too imprecise to afford simultaneity. How do I weigh one afternoon against the other?

The watch's face marks out time according to the unit of the day. A day is linear in time. Tuesday follows Monday, and it is, in turn, succeeded by Wednesday. Tuesday is not the same as Monday; its texture and activities are different. A day also marks a cyclical time. One Wednesday is not always clearly distinguishable from another. The day accordingly affords what Bryony Randall has termed 'a background of repetition, of the same coming round again and again' (2007: 161). The structure of dailiness enables us to organize experience, either by contrasting our own experience of one day with another – a Monday with a Tuesday, for example, or this Wednesday and last Wednesday – or by comparing our own Sunday with somebody else's experience of the same day. Suicide stands out against, and seems inassimilable to, the rhythm and regularity of the day.

In what I have described, suicide emerges as the extraordinary. It comes into definition in and through its distinction from the everyday. It is the exceptional moment, the catastrophe that shocks us out of our habitual routines. Yet suicide unsettles not (or not only) because it breaks or shatters the everyday but also (or rather) because it does not: the clock keeps on ticking. To conceptualize suicide, then, we might helpfully turn to those critics who have challenged a binary divide between the extraordinary and the everyday. Tia DeNora argues that such a dichotomy 'may prevent us from appreciating the admixture of "special" and "routine" in all aspects of our lives' (2014: xix). For Rita Felski, the extraordinary should not be extrapolated from the everyday, given that 'every life contains epiphanic moments, experiences of trauma, and points of departure from mundane routines' (2000: 92). Felski urges us to think, rather, about how the everyday and the non-everyday are interwoven. Suicide would not, then, be incommensurable with the mundane reality of a Monday or a Tuesday. It would take shape in shuttling between the ordinary act of folding the clothes and the extraordinary act of swallowing the pills, in an attitude of alertness to the imbrication of the former in the latter and of the latter in the former.

In *Mrs. Dalloway*, Virginia Woolf posed the question of how the suicide of Septimus Smith could be narrated as part of the ongoing rhythms and pulsations of a 'matter-of-fact' ([1925] 2000: 33) Wednesday in June. The problem resolved itself into one of form: what shape might Woolf give to her novel, such that it could accommodate the daily life of Septimus, of Clarissa Dalloway and of numerous other characters as they moved around London? Woolf's solution was to structure her narrative according to the chronology of a single day with the clock face of Big Ben marking out the passing hours. Time is sounded out in the chimes of Big Ben that ripple through the city; as their 'leaden circles dissolv[e] in the air' ([1925] 2000: 4), they disperse into the thoughts and preoccupations of the characters, revealing the multiple temporalities through which the everyday is experienced and inhabited. The narrative shuttles between the clock time of Big Ben and time as it is subjectively experienced. As Randall outlines, Woolf's point is not simply that the everyday reality of the individual fluctuates between clock time and internal time but also that time, through the simultaneous perception of Big Ben's chimes, enables us to connect our own experience with that of others; the narrative device 'allow[s] for a communion and communication, whether direct or indirect, between characters' (2007: 160). The death of Septimus is untimely, a tear in the fabric of Clarissa's party, but it is also woven into the lives of the other characters. The exceptionalism of suicide is mitigated by Woolf, as Septimus's act is folded into the quotidian rituals of an unremarkable Wednesday in June.

In 'Modern Fiction' ([1925] 1984), Woolf famously called attention to the importance for the writer of attending to the ordinary:

Examine for a moment an ordinary mind on an ordinary day. The mind receives a myriad impressions – trivial, fantastic, evanescent, or engraved with the sharpness of steel. From all sides they come, an incessant shower of innumerable atoms; and as they fall, as they shape themselves into the life of Monday or Tuesday, the accent falls differently from of old; the moment of importance came not here but there. ... Let us record the atoms as they fall upon the mind in the order in which they fall, let us trace the pattern.

([1925] 1984: 160–1)

In this passage, Woolf conceives of the day – the Monday or Tuesday – as a vessel that holds and gives shape to the innumerable impressions that fall upon the mind. The day both gives form to these impressions and is itself a form, like the novel, that can order and make sense of experience. Randall has rightly observed that Woolf oscillates in this passage between 'randomness ... and structure' (2007: 157). The Woolfian day is likewise suspended between form and formlessness, unity and dissolution. The task of the novelist is to decide where the accent will fall. Woolf is primarily concerned with a modernist attention to those moments in the day that would, in the nineteenth-century novel, have passed unremarked: our half-conscious habits and routines. My interest in what follows lies in where the accent falls in *Mrs. Dalloway* between the ordinary event of Clarissa buying flowers and the extraordinary moment of Septimus's death. What pattern does Woolf trace between and across them?

Mrs. Dalloway opens with Clarissa's departure from the house to buy the flowers for the party herself. Stepping into the freshness of the June morning, Clarissa also steps back in time to memories of summers spent at Bourton in the company of long-dispersed friends, who will be gathered together once more at her party that evening: 'What a lark! What a plunge! For so it had always seemed to her when, with a little squeak of the hinges, which she could hear now, she had burst open the French windows and plunged at Bourton into the open air' ([1925] 2000: 3). Woolf immediately plunges the reader into an ordinary task – the running of an errand – that is simultaneously heightened, charged with a sensory and mnemonic intensity. When the backfiring of a car sounds out like a 'pistol' ([1925] 2000: 14) on Bond Street, everyday routine is further intensified, as a visit to the flower shop momentarily threatens to transform into a plunge towards death. Death, when it does eventually catch up with Clarissa in the news of Septimus's suicide at her party, also takes the form of the plunge through a window. As Dr Bradshaw arrived to commit the young man into his care, Septimus opened 'the large Bloomsbury lodging-house window' ([1925] 2000: 163) and plunged downward, '[flinging] himself vigorously, violently down on to Mrs Filmer's area railings' ([1925] 2000: 164). These two moments of opening a window and plunging outside frame the novel, and, through them, Woolf asks where the accent of this particular day should fall.

Do we accord more value to the plunge to death than to the plunge into life? Certainly, the former is more visible than the latter. Septimus's plunge onto the railings summons the ambulance to clear what remains of his body while Clarissa's plunge into life registers only as a pause in her step.

Although Septimus encounters a range of characters in the novel, he does not come into direct contact with Clarissa. The first connection between Clarissa and Septimus is one of simultaneity. The narrator identifies each of their actions as Big Ben strikes midday, prompting the reader to consider the relation between them:

> It was precisely twelve o'clock; twelve by Big Ben; whose stroke was wafted over the northern part of London; blent with that of other clocks, mixed in a thin ethereal way with the clouds and wisps of smoke and died up there among the seagulls – twelve o'clock struck as Clarissa Dalloway laid her green dress on her bed, and the Warren Smiths walked down Harley Street. Twelve was the hour of their appointment.
>
> ([1925] 2000: 103)

Clarissa's laying aside of the dress that she is mending signifies her submission to medical authority, which mirrors that of Septimus as he walks to his appointment with Dr Bradshaw. Since her recent influenza, which has left her with a weakened heart, Clarissa's daily life has been punctuated by a retreat into her bedroom at midday to rest. Clarissa is a survivor of the influenza pandemic; Septimus is a veteran of the recent war. The everyday life of each character reflects the experience from which they have barely emerged. The ordinary day in 1923, Woolf implies, is marked not only by contact with the war, which has left visible traces such as the Cenotaph in the city, but also by contact with the influenza pandemic, which has left its own affective residues in London that register as an atmosphere of febrile intensity.[5]

The war has left Septimus with gaping holes in his experience of temporality, rents that open up in the fabric of the everyday and through which his dead friend Evans steps to greet him. Clarissa's influenza has also been experienced as a tear in the flow of time, which materializes in her accelerated ageing process: her illness has left her hair 'almost white' ([1925] 2000: 39). Clarissa's decision to mend her dress, torn at an Embassy party, represents a series of simple actions, like buying the flowers, that for Liesl Olson 'make up the substance of the novel' and that 'dominate – even hold in check – moments of anxiety' (2003: 49). Clarissa is soothed by the rhythmic motion of her sewing, 'her needle, drawing the silk smoothly to its gentle pause' ([1995] 2000: 43). She is comforted, too, by assembling from her workbox the various objects required for the task: 'her silks, her scissors, her – what was it? – her thimble, of course' ([1925] 2000: 41). Septimus is also temporarily restored by his wife, Rezia's, sewing, as she makes a hat for Mrs. Peters. Assembling the materials for the hat reconnects Septimus to Rezia and to his former self: he sorts through her workbox for 'ribbons and beads, tassels, artificial flowers' ([1925] 2000: 157). But if Clarissa's sewing leads to the assembling of her party, Septimus quickly loses hold of the everyday reality that the materials and fabrics represent. Olson aptly describes his suicide as 'his final disassembling, a turning away from what – in this afternoon scene – he briefly embraces' (2003: 55).

Clarissa's mending of her dress anticipates her later repair of the tear in the party, caused by the news of Septimus's death. Clarissa's initial response on hearing of the young man's suicidal leap is to experience her own plunge towards death once more, through an intense identification with Septimus's final act: 'He had killed himself – but how? Always her body went through it first, when she was told, suddenly, of an accident; her dress flamed, her body burnt. He had thrown himself from a window. Up had flashed the ground; through him, blundering, bruising, went the rusty spikes' ([1925] 2000: 201–2). Although the emphasis is on Septimus's fall, Clarissa's association with burning recalls the fever of her influenza – the suicide is not entirely separable from Clarissa's own recent plunge towards death. Clarissa retreats to her attic room, the space of her confinement, to gather herself as she had earlier gathered the silk of the dress with her thread. She watches an old lady in a room opposite, preparing to go to bed alone. Clarissa sees in her a figure for her own death, which will be quiet, restrained, almost indiscernible, like turning out a light in a room. There is a trace of envy in Clarissa's thoughts of Septimus as she 'felt glad that he had done it; thrown it away while they went on living' ([1925] 2000: 204). As Big Ben chimes the hour, Clarissa returns to 'assemble' her party ([1925] 2000: 204). In an act that reprises her first stepping out into the day, she 'came in from the little room' ([1925] 2000: 204), plunging back into life once more. Olson sees in this ending 'an affirmation of the ordinary, not the traumatic' (2003: 56) but the ordinary to which Clarissa returns has been marked by its encounter with suicide. The ending is a disclosure of the proximity between the ordinary and the exceptional: the necessary intertwining of the two.

Elizabeth Outka has identified *Mrs. Dalloway* as integral to a 'viral modernism' (2020: 2), a cluster of literary texts that register 'in gaps, silences, atmospheres, fragments, and hidden bodies' (2020: 2) the affective afterlife of the influenza pandemic. Outka observes that 'the aftermath of a pandemic outbreak registers differently than a war, changing everything yet lying apart from the more structured, visible histories left by more public battles' (2020: 123). This distinction can be mapped onto the bodies of Clarissa and Septimus. Clarissa's invisible heart condition contrasts with the visibility of Septimus's suicide. Septimus's plunge mangles his body and makes visible the damage that has been inflicted on him by war while Clarissa's influenza evades visible representation. It is glimpsed only in its shaping of her movements and perceptions.[6] Septimus's death becomes legible *as* suicide through the violence of its enactment: the impact of the railings onto which he throws himself signifies the force of his intention to die. I return to the visibility of violence on the body as an important, if problematically gendered, signifier of suicidal intentionality in Chapter 2.

Through Clarissa, Woolf asks how suicide falls onto an ordinary mind in an ordinary day. Woolf does not avoid the violence of Septimus's death. She makes clear the material damage it inflicts on his body. But Woolf does not prioritize the singular moment of Septimus's death over the ways in which his suicide shapes, and takes shape among, the living. Septimus's suicide creates affective reverberations that ripple out concentrically across the city, like the chimes of Big Ben. Suicide takes on an unexpected sociality in the novel as it is variously perceived, narrated and interpreted over the course of the day. We learn not only of Clarissa's reaction but also of Rezia's, Bradshaw's and the other guests' at the party. Suicide describes not only the moment of Septimus's death but how the news of his death is received, passed on and understood – how, in other words, it is related. This insight is also central to Jocelyn Lim Chua's ethnographic study of suicide in the southern Indian state of Kerala, where reported suicide rates have been double or triple the national average since the 1990s. At the heart of Chua's book is an attempt to understand suicide 'not in the anonymous terms of a suicide epidemic but on the scale of the individual case' (2014: 10). She speaks to the various people who have contact with, and transmit news of, a death by suicide: family, friends, neighbours of the deceased, police officers, doctors, journalists. Her conversations unravel how we collectively live beside suicide, as an ongoing material, psychic and social presence. Chua's ethnographic witnessing is one mode of relating suicide's 'descent into the ordinary' (2014: 23), and Lisa

Relating Suicide

Stevenson's anthropological work in the Canadian Arctic also testifies to the efficacy of such embedded approaches. Building on Andrew Bennett's (2017) analysis of suicide in the work of James Joyce, my reading of *Mrs. Dalloway* indicates that the modernist novel can also relate suicide, as it is simultaneously, but differently, lived by those who encounter it and as it shapes itself into the ordinary life of a Monday or a Tuesday.

In the nick of time

Two clocks hang on the wall of my kitchen. I consult the larger of the two when I am checking the time, and my glance habitually moves across to the smaller clock. It is a tide clock, and high and low water are inscribed on its face at twelve and six o' clock (Figure 4). I can see when the ebb tide will reach low water or when the flood tide will reach the high-water mark. I have set the clock according to the tide table for Crosby beach, a place towards which I am inclined and to which I will take you in Chapter 3. I orient myself between and across these two clocks. The larger keeps me on time. The smaller reminds me that there is another temporality that also gives me my bearings.

I do not know whether my sister consulted the tide tables before she walked into the sea. Had my tide clock been set to the Stray on the afternoon that she died, I imagine that its hand would have been at twelve o'clock, showing the high-water point as it gave way to the ebb tide. My sister's body was found a few hours at most after she entered the water, floating in the shallows as the sea retreated down the sands. The tidal current flows south from the Stray, but her body was washed up just a few metres from where she had walked into the sea.

After leaving the family home, my sister caught a bus and a train out to the coast. I picture her looking at her watch as she walked from the bus stop to the train station, to check that she would make her connection. My image of the early afternoon remains in sharp focus; I have made the same journey often enough. The scene becomes more blurred once my sister arrived at the beach. I reason she would have bided her time, but my sister would not have been able to hesitate for long because early evening would have brought the dog walkers out after supper. This is mere supposition, though. My sister might have walked directly from the train into the sea, or she may have wavered, not sure that she would see her plan through to the end. The next fixed temporal point is eight o'clock that evening when a dog walker – or, more accurately, his dog – found my sister's body in the water.

Olivia Stevenson has argued that we should be more attentive to the suicidal journey, the movements of those intending to commit suicide. Stevenson challenges the prevailing perception of this journey as a 'linear continuum' (2016: 194), which entails that 'suicidal persons ... mov[e] from points A to B, with a singular goal being death' (2016: 193). Stevenson contends that the journey to suicide is less predictable and more adaptive than this, 'a dynamic amalgam of felt stresses, thoughts, intentions, preparations, executions, and decision-making' (2016: 194). It is more pragmatic, and more ordinary, than we often assume. We work back from the end point. In so doing, Stevenson indicates, we close off the multiple possible directions that the suicidal journey might, and could, have taken.

Stevenson refers to the hours immediately preceding an intended suicide. Too often, she contends, suicide prevention is seen to be a matter of diverting the suicidal journey at the critical moment, acting in the nick of time to interrupt or change its course. Stevenson finds this line of reasoning problematic, in that it accords no agency to the suicidal individual, who fails to register as '[a] thinking, feeling and changing subject' (2016: 194). Responsiveness to the suicidal individual's evolving thoughts and intentions is replaced by an exclusive focus on the actions of those around her.

I propose to linger with the unpredictable and impromptu time of the suicidal journey. This temporality rubs against, and is in friction with, the time frame of the plan. The plan is defined by Grosz as a mechanism of limitation: 'the attempt to foreclose certain options ... the cutting off of future openings, a technique of elimination, the giving in advance of a future that has yet to be made' (2004: 215). The plan closes off the emergent, that which is in the process of becoming. What might it mean to restore to the suicidal journey the temporality of its own unique unfolding? This entails imagining an uncertain present, in which the future is not yet known. In Grosz's terms, it opens up a 'nick' in time, the cut or tear that allows 'multiple futures' to be realized, and that envisages 'open pathways' rather than a fixed or determined course (2004: 253). In admitting a range of possible endings, this approach expands the suicidal act beyond the experiences of those who die to encompass those who survive a suicide attempt or intention.

Can the suicidal journey be reconceived, not as a path to be followed but as an orientation? Ahmed has observed that the path is a line already marked out in advance: 'We can see the path as a trace of past journeys, made out of footprints, traces of feet that tread and in treading create a line on the ground. ... Lines are both created by being followed and are followed by being created' (2006a: 544). The path captures our prevailing tendency to work back from the death, retracing the steps that led to that point. We are looking, in Ahmed's terms, for the line on the ground. Orientation is future-facing and, while it entails turning in a particular direction, it can always alter its course: 'If orientations point us to the future, to what we are moving toward, then they also keep open the possibility of changing directions, of finding other paths' (2006a: 569). What might it mean to read the suicidal journey as a mode of orientation, to conceive it as a tending toward, rather than as a fixed destination?[7]

In *To the River*, Olivia Laing poses this question in relation to the suicide of Virginia Woolf. From the very first sentences of her book, Laing is preoccupied with the question of orientation, with how we find our bearings at times of change or crisis. She defines herself as someone who inclines towards water, and who is drawn to the River Ouse in Sussex, 'a river I've returned to over and again, in sickness and in health, in grief, in desolation and in joy' (2012: 3). Having recently lost a job and a relationship, Laing directs her course to the river, hoping that it will re-orient her, set her back on course.

Laing identifies Woolf, and identifies herself with Woolf, as a companion writer who is also oriented towards water and who famously drowned herself in the Ouse on 28 March 1941. Laing notes of Woolf's notably fluid vocabulary, 'she writes of *plunging, flooding, going under, being submerged*' (2012: 10). These are Woolf's favoured metaphors for describing her creative process, and they reflect the psychoanalytic milieu in which she was immersed. A tide of such imagery courses through the novels – the title of Laing's book riffs on *To the Lighthouse* (1927), and *The Waves* (1931) was the last of Woolf's novels to be published before her death.[8] The reader is left to question whether, and how, to relate Woolf's preoccupation with water to her eventual drowning. In Laing's eloquent words: 'What is one to make of this great weight of waters?' (2012: 195).

Orientation affords Laing a means of resisting the pull of 'hindsight', that backward glance which would 'weight every word with what would take place, years later, in the Ouse' (2012: 195). Laing's frustrated attempt to identify the place where the river begins provides a valuable early lesson: 'It's not always possible to plot where something starts. If I went down on my knees amid the fallen leaves, I would not find the exact spot where the Ouse began, where a trickle of rain gathered sufficient momentum to make it to the coast' (2012: 18). Laing is similarly reluctant to plot Woolf's suicide to a singular source or origin. To look back from the outcome is, she notes, to 'see events inflected with a meaning that the one who lived them never grasped' (2012: 199). It imposes a false coherence, which distorts and belies the lived experience – an evanescent daily reality to which, as we have already seen, Woolf herself was particularly attentive. Laing takes her cue from the river, finding in its shift and flux, its glint and glimmer, a figure for 'that uncertain, glancing quality that is the hallmark of the present' (2012: 200). The Ouse, Laing discovers, does not run in a straight line from source to sea but meanders, eddies, gathers into pools and wanders into creeks. It is inclined towards the sea, but it can alter its path and branch off course. The river speaks of adaptability and contingency, of a course that shifts and changes. I have already noted that Septimus's pleasure in Rezia's hat-making suggests that the June day recorded in *Mrs. Dalloway* could have ended differently without the arrival of Bradshaw. So, in Woolf's final writing, Laing observes indications of an alternative path that might have been taken by Woolf herself: in the last diary entries 'gladness – *aliveness* – bubbles periodically through' (2012: 207).

Laing's book contains an undertow that I find more troubling, however. Her reflections on surface and depth form a cross-current that tugs at her writing on Woolf's suicide, pulling it in a different direction. Laing describes her youthful habit of swimming in the Ouse at Southsea – where Woolf's body was recovered from the water – in a 'current that threatened to tumble me beneath the surface and bowl me clean to the sea' (2012: 4). There is an attraction to the depths, and Woolf emerges for Laing as a muse who 'possessed … a gift for descending beneath the surface of the world' (2012: 10). Woolf's preoccupation with water becomes darker, more threatening, and a line – albeit tentative – is drawn from her early 'effortless plunges' under the surface to the later 'vanishing act of a far more sinister sort' (2012: 10).

This aspect of Laing's writing is problematic on her own terms because of its freighting of the present with the weight of what is not yet known. There is also a gendered opposition between surface and depth such that the surface equates to a masculine consciousness and reason, while the depths represent an unconscious, corporeal and feminine realm. The suicide of a woman by drowning is a vanishing act of an altogether different kind, as the dead become submerged beneath a tide of cultural imagery that equates women, drowning and madness. Woolf's specifically female body comes to matter in how her suicide is understood and interpreted by Laing. Woolf's death is narrated as her gradual descent beneath the surface of reason so that she was no longer able to emerge from the depths. Woolf's suicidal journey follows the well-trodden path of women who succumb to madness, and

Laing, somewhat predictably, invokes Sylvia Plath and Ophelia when she walks the stretch of the Ouse where Woolf died.

Laing's description of the Brooks, the marshy reclaimed lowland where Woolf entered the Ouse, creates a mythological watery realm. As Laing enters the Brooks her thoughts take 'a ghoulish turn', focusing on 'the doomed woman, the lost lover' (2012: 189). She searches for 'omens', and a cormorant dives into the river, 'a creature that can fly through two elements' (2012: 189). As Laing pursues her riparian course, she, too, is similarly suspended between water and air. She feels as if she has 'fallen to the bottom of a glass dome' (2012: 190). In this enchanted sphere, walking assumes the 'buoyancy' (2012: 190) of swimming, and the river is no longer distinguishable from the path:

> The path stretched on before me, almost flush with the ruffled water. … There was something very strange about walking aside such brimful water, as if I could step down onto it and continue along that shifting track. The river was completely opaque now, aglint with borrowed light, its surface coloured the bluish-green of spilled petrol, teased by the wind and current into tufts and crests and little waves.
>
> (2012: 191)

Laing evokes the place of Woolf's death as magically blending air and water, surface and depth, with the cormorant its guardian and tutelary spirit. Woolf's drowning is transformed by this place, soothed and eased. It is figured as the step that Laing could – but does not – take from path to shifting track. The landscape becomes the agent in Laing's description, enticing and disarming.

The Brooks is a couple of miles across the fields from Woolf's home at Rodmell, and it is also within sight of Asheham, where Woolf rented a house in which she spent her wedding night and finished her first novel. Woolf, Laing observes, 'loved walking in this marsh' (2012: 189). It was a place to which she often came and in which she found her bearings. Viewed from Woolf's, rather than from Laing's, perspective, Woolf's choice to enter the river here is not only a pragmatic decision – it is a short walk from the house – but also a relational one. It connects her to a landscape she loves and to a place that is imbued with memories. The Brooks is a working landscape, criss-crossed with 'ditches', 'sewers' and 'sluice gates' (2012: 189). Read without the benefit of hindsight, the place where Woolf drowns seems more quotidian and everyday than eerie and enchanted.

Her decision to die there accords with Olivia Stevenson's observation that suicidal journeys are commonly 'bound up in *ordinary* places' (2016: 201). Suicidal individuals gravitate towards common places: 'park benches, car parks, copses of trees, streets' (2016: 201). Places of suicide are often oriented towards others, either in their personal association or in their public-facing location.

My sister loved to be at the Stray. It was, in practical terms, the closest stretch of coast to the family home. It was, and still is, a resolutely industrial place, overshadowed by the remains of the steelworks and the port on the mouth of the River Tees. It was densely layered for my sister with memories and associations. We spent many days on the beach, spotting birds and collecting shells and pebbles. She loved to walk there with a friend and his dogs. If I try to bring the beach on that late August afternoon into sharper focus, I imagine my sister walking along the Stray to where the groynes begin, calling to mind the people she loved. Even if these memories were not enough to change her orientation, to redirect her steps back up the beach and to prevent her from setting her course to the shimmering line of the horizon, she chose to die in a place where she was surrounded by the company they afforded.

When Woolf's body was recovered from the Ouse, the policeman, Collins, reported that her watch had stopped at 11.45 a.m., which was, Laing notes, 'a good hour and a quarter before Leonard … had found the letters she'd left for him in the upstairs sitting room at Monk's House and run pell-mell through the Brooks to find her' (2012: 206).[9] The stopped watch meant there was an exact time of death. It established that Woolf had written her suicide letters, walked through the fields to the Brooks and entered the river, without diverting from her course. There was a clear and uninterrupted line of action, and the coroner's verdict at the inquest was suicide. The cause of death was recorded as 'immersion in the river … by her own act so killing herself, while the balance of her mind was disturbed' (2012: 206).[10]

My sister's death certificate records her cause of death to be drowning with an open verdict. At the coronial inquest, the imprecise time of her death, sometime between late afternoon and early evening, meant an uninterrupted line could not be drawn between point A and point B: her departure from the house and her death. There was time unaccounted for, which meant that the possibility of death by accident or misadventure could not be ruled out. My sister had taken her time. Or time itself had not been taken and recorded. Either way, there was no linear continuum.[11] There were gaps in the narrative, which could not be filled in. My sister's death could not be named as suicide partly because of this temporal ambiguity. The open verdict has remained, for me, a source of continued unease. My sister's death did not count as suicide; it was not counted in the statistics. Katrina Jaworski has observed that we should give serious attention 'not only to *what* we know of suicide but also to *how* we know what we know of suicide' (2014: 156). Suicide is not self-evident but requires the production of evidence. The materialization of suicide – or its failure to materialize – as coronial verdict, can rest on as little, or as much, as whether a watch stops when it is immersed in water.[12]

The opening up of the suicidal journey to unpredictability, uncertainty and hesitation matters because it has material effects. What we think we know about suicide is that it follows a singular path or course. We have come to know this because this is how suicide is named and recognized in legal discourse. I have suggested that this is too narrow and restricted a definition of the suicidal journey. It fails to register as suicide those intentional deaths which do not fit within its parameters – those that fluctuate or that falter in their course. Neither does it recognize those suicidal journeys that do not end in death. There is a pressing need to relate, and to listen to, different stories of suicide – stories that challenge us to reflect on how our understanding of suicide is shaped and with what effects. In understanding and recognizing suicide, might we be better served by looking beyond the retrospective view, which works back from the death, reorienting ourselves instead towards the untimely, the discontinuous and the open-ended?

Notes

1   Denise Riley has reflected on what her experience of maternal loss might share in common with other forms of bereavement, observing of the support group that she attended: 'I think I was the only one who was the mother of somebody who had quite literally walked out of my house and not come back. And was never seen again by me' (Baraitser, 2020: 342). Riley's description of a loss in which the deceased leaves the house and is not seen alive again resonates with many experiences of bereavement by suicide.

2   Judith Butler has called attention to the hybrid form in which Riley writes *Time Lived*, describing her lyrical essay as a work that 'wrestles with description, the poetic, the philosophical, the relation of sound to sequence, the strains on syntax as we know it' (2020: 332). Through these varied formal resources, Butler argues, Riley's essay continually 'pull[s] back' from the 'conclusion' of indescribability (2020: 331).

3   Katrina Jaworski and Daniel G. Scott likewise consider poetry to be an apt
     form for representing suicide because it 'refracts sequential thought', and
     because its acoustic resonances set in play 'sympathetic vibrations' that help us
     'to feel something without having the words to describe it' (2020: 579).

4   Jaworski and Scott note that contemporary suicide research has charted
     the time of day that suicide most often occurs (between 6 a.m. and 4 p.m.),
     the time of the week (between Monday and Thursday), the time of the year
     (between spring and early summer), and its correlation with special occasions
     such as birthdays and public holidays. In each instance, they note, '[t]hese
     studies treat time as a causal factor that charts the temporal distribution of
     suicide', rather than asking 'how time contributes to making sense of the
     inexpressible or ineffable in suicide' (2020: 578).

5   The influenza pandemic lasted from February 1918 until April 1920. Woolf was
     left with a weakened heart from her infection.

6   Outka traces Septimus's suicide to the influenza pandemic, the symptoms of
     which included 'violent derangement, hallucinations, and suicidal depression'
     (2020: 126). I distinguish between Septimus as a survivor of the war and
     Clarissa as a survivor of the pandemic, contrasting the (hyper)visibility of the
     suicidal act and the invisibility of the chronic symptoms caused by influenza.

7   Saartje Tack has turned to Ahmed's work on orientation to pursue a different
     line of argument in relation to suicide. Tack's interest lies in the emphasis
     on suicide prevention across suicidology and critical suicidology, which is,
     she argues, underpinned by a presumption 'that the desire to live is a natural
     characteristic of bodies' (2019: 47). For Tack, rather, the subject who desires
     to live 'comes into being through a wide range of regulatory technologies
     that in/trans/form bodily being-in-the-world' (2019: 47). Ahmed's concept
     of orientation, here referring to the orientation towards life, enables Tack
     to examine 'the sedimented effects of prior orientations, of history, of
     somatechnics' (2019: 51) which produce the alignment towards life as
     normative, as well as the 'straightening devices' that realign the suicidal subject
     who has become 'disorientated toward death' (2019: 52).

8   Woolf's final novel, *Between the Acts*, was published shortly after her death
     in 1941.

9   Woolf left behind three suicide letters, two of which were addressed to
     Leonard and one to her sister Vanessa Bell. Her letters articulated her fear of
     an impending mental breakdown and the burden which this would place on
     others.

10   The coronial verdict at once grants Woolf intentionality and removes the
     capacity for decision-making from her. Simon Critchley notes that this paradox
     is symptomatic of English coronial law: 'If suicide is a free act, made "in one's
     senses", then it is an offense to God, King and country; if suicide is adjudged to
     have taken place with diminished responsibility or some form of mental illness
     like severe depression, then freedom is eliminated. Either way, the moral,

philosophical and existential space for the consideration of suicide as a free act is closed down' (2015: 28).

11 In *Life? Or Theatre?* (1940–1942), Charlotte Salomon painted her aunt's suicidal journey across Berlin to drown herself in a lake. Maria Stepanova's description of the painting encapsulates the equation between intention and a continuous, unbroken line of action: 'Here's a woman leaving her home on her way to end her life. Eighteen little figures repeating across the page in different phases of movement, a little like a corridor with *intention* moving down it. Each following figure confirms the decision of the one before, each new figure moves a step closer to the hole in the ice' (2021: 189–90). Griselda Pollock's reading of the same image is closer to my own emphasis on the uncertain outcome of the unfolding event. For Pollock, Salomon's figuring of her aunt's suicidal journey through the repeated figures enacts 'a self-questioning, sustained over the trajectory of the young woman's departure from home and arrival at her watery grave many kilometres from that home' (2018: 133).

12 The materialization of suicide here is also a question of technology: my sister's watch could only capture time, but a smartwatch would also have captured her heartbeat, the surrounding temperature and her location, which would have enabled a line to be drawn connecting point A to point B.

Figure 3 My sister, the Stray, Redcar, 1988. Photograph © the author

2
HOW?

Drowning in cliché

> The following afternoon, on receiving the news of [my mother's]
> death, I flew to Austria. The plane was half empty; it was a steady,
> quiet flight, the air clear and cloudless, the lights of changing cities
> far below. Reading the paper, drinking beer, looking out the window,
> I gradually sank into a tired, impersonal sense of well-being. Yes,
> I thought over and over again, carefully enunciating my thoughts to
> myself: THAT DOES IT. THAT DOES IT. THAT DOES IT. GOOD.
> GOOD. GOOD.
>
> (Handke, [1972] 2012: 63)

I am arrested by Peter Handke's description of his response to his mother's
suicide on two counts. First, I am drawn to that quiet word, 'impersonal',
which is almost lost in the surprise of the word 'well-being' that follows.
Impersonal is a vital, if enigmatic, qualifier of that word. What does it mean
for a sense of well-being to be impersonal? How does this question relate
to the second aspect of this passage that stops me in my tracks, namely the
thoughts that Handke goes on to articulate? Less thoughts than discrete
words or phrases, these capitalized enunciations sound repeatedly in
Handke's head. They do not really say anything, and neither do they lead
anywhere. Rather, they are the kind of clichéd expressions that we utter when
there is a need for something to be said, but when we are self-consciously
filling a gap. Like the flight, which conveys Handke from where he was when
he heard of his mother's suicide to her home in Austria, these words mark a
passage between things.

In the days after my sister's death, an equivalent phrase echoed through
my thoughts: 'She's really gone and done it now.' At once familiar, true and
wholly inadequate, these formulaic words had surfaced out of childhood.
They gave my thoughts something concrete to hold on to. The phrase was
a first intimation that to be bereaved by suicide is to enter what Yiyun Li

has aptly described as 'cliché-land' (2019: 9). Faced with suicide, thought operates in and through cliché. Communication with others also takes the form of cliché, as nobody – including the bereaved – knows the right or the wrong thing to say. Suicide is arguably more susceptible to cliché than other deaths because the dead vanish into the cliché of their final act when the intense privacy of their ending is turned over to the public gaze. In this section, I dwell for a time in cliché-land in order to ask what work it might do in the immediate aftermath of a suicide. I am interested in cliché as a linguistic mode in which meaning is not so much substantive as performative. As a communal form of expression, cliché may not actually state all that much, but it can still say a great deal about language as a form of sociality.

Yiyun Li wrote *Where Reasons End* immediately following her son's suicide.[1] The novel takes the form of an imagined conversation between mother and son, as Li invents a world in which the living and the dead might be together again. The discussion between the narrator and Nikolai – one of many names that Li's son used to call himself – captures a tone of bickering affection, and it centres on how language is 'relearned' (2019: 138) in the wake of suicide. This is not a declaration of language's failure to convey the reality of suicide. Instead, Li takes as her starting point the clichés that impinge upon the life of the bereaved:

> I was a generic parent grieving a generic child lost to an inexplicable tragedy. Already there were three clichés. I could wage my personal war against each one of them. Grieve: from Latin *gravare*, to burden, and *gravis*, grave, heavy. What kind of mother would consider it a burden to live in the vacancy left by a child? Explicate: from Latin *ex* (out) + *plicare* (fold), to unfold. But calling Nikolai's act inexplicable was like calling a migrant bird ending on a new continent lost. Who can say that the vagrant doesn't have a reason to change the course of its flight? Nothing inexplicable for me – only I didn't want to explain. A mother's job is to enfold, not to unfold.
>
> Tragedy: Now that is an inexplicable word. What was a goat song, after all, which is what tragedy seemed to mean originally?
>
> (2019: 5)

Li unfolds the exact meaning of words, by tracing out their etymologies, in order to enfold her loss. The words she is given – grieving, inexplicable, tragedy – are washed out, faded: they are not up to the job that they are being asked to do. Li's explication of the word grief as an act of carrying registers that mourning for her son is not a melancholic burden; she will carry her son in death as she had formerly carried him in pregnancy. 'We once gave Nikolai a life of flesh and blood', she observes, 'and I'm doing it over again, this time by words' (2019: 64).

Li speaks to her son of the clichés that people have written to her in letters of condolence, out of 'helplessness, awkwardness, or politeness' (2019: 99). Adults, she tells Nikolai, have become stuck in the fact of his death, remembering the suicidal act rather than the person: 'They ask, How could that happen? What went wrong? Or, they say things to the effect that in the direst situation there is a bright side if we let words like love and hope work their magic' (2019: 101). Nikolai's adolescent friends do not have the same sense of constraint. In their condolence letters, Nikolai is remembered as one of them and is animated once again:

> A friend of Nikolai's had written, reminiscing that when they stood in a circle to talk, he bounced up and down as though he had springs in his shoes. Another friend had told me that when they had gone out for walks, he would jump into the air to pick the plums that were out of everyone's reach. … How can one make a monument, granite or marble or bronze, lithe and nimble in flight?
>
> (2019: 137–8)

Nikolai's friends (re)animate Li's son as he was in life, finding words to speak of him that reach beyond the conventional phrases of consolation.

I have placed at the head of this chapter a photograph I took of my sister ten years before her death (Figure 3). We are on the Stray, not far from where her body was found. She is walking away from me, striding out across the sands to the low-water mark. When I look at the image, I see again my sister's distinctive gait, purposeful and decisive. Yet the photograph is overlaid with my knowledge of her suicide, which turns it – or, more precisely, my gaze upon it – into a cliché of melancholic remembrance. My sister becomes the punctum, a detail which bears witness to the death that could not be discerned at the time the photograph was taken. Shot on an inexpensive camera, the indistinctness of the photograph heightens the sense of a life that is already in the process of being erased. Mandy Bloomfield has noted of the material qualities of reproduced images, 'the deteriorations of the medium … indexically register a process of disintegration and distancing that materially amplifies the effect of … loss' (2016: 100). Like Li, I am left wondering how to remember the dead without tumbling, time and again, into cliché land.

One way forward is to work with cliché rather than against it. The photograph of my sister forms one of a series I took on that day. Arranged in order, the sequence anticipates my sister's final disappearance: her retreating figure becomes smaller and smaller until she appears as a speck of white barely visible on the tideline (Figure 5). I can also play the sequence in reverse so that my sister advances towards me across the sand, coming back into definition and focus. George Szirtes played a comparable conjuring trick in *The Photographer at Sixteen*, a memoir of his mother which begins with her death in the back of an ambulance after she has taken an overdose. Szirtes's difficulty in knowing what to feel when he learns of his mother's suicide stems from not knowing much of his mother's life. Szirtes's memoir rewinds his mother's life from death to birth, like watching a film backwards, using photographs from the family album. His gesture is at once one of reparation, attending to his mother in death as he had not been able to in life, and of recuperation. Although we know the ending of the story, its actors do not, and Szirtes highlights both the contingencies of history and his parents' ignorance of what was yet to come: 'None of this, as they say, was meant to happen. It is only we, we gods of time and space, who know their future' (2019: 5). In making the reader complicit in his knowledge of what was to come, Szirtes embraces the cliché of the melancholic retrospective gaze, using it to return 'to a … beginning where all is innocence and potential' (2019: 5).[2] His memoir creates a nick in time, resisting suicide's teleological drive towards closure by giving back to his mother the multiplicity of directions that her own life could possibly have taken.

Li's narrator has moved house since her son's death, and she tells Nikolai of a persistent, rhythmic noise which seemed to come from inside the new house. It turned out that a bird was knocking repeatedly on the basement window. The conversation unfolds as follows:

> It's just a bird, he said.
> And a window, and a house, and a season, I said.
> For sure you're not a connoisseur of nouns, he said.
> A life's story can be told by the simplest nouns, I said.
>
> (2019: 81)

Turning to more troublesome nouns – loss, grief and sorrow – Li considers that, like window and house, these words 'frame this life, as solid as the ceiling and the floor and the walls and the doors' (2019: 93). Together, they mark out a space that we inhabit. Li's foregrounding of the conversation between mother and son reinforces that it is in language that the bereaved must renegotiate their relation to the dead. It is a cliché that the recently bereaved expect at any moment to hear the deceased's key turning in the lock. In the wake of Woolf's suicide, Leonard observed of living at Monk's House without her:

> I know that V. will not come across the garden from the Lodge, and yet I look in that direction for her. I know that she is drowned and yet I listen for her to come in at the door. I know that it is the last page and yet I turn it over. There is no limit to one's stupidity and selfishness.
>
> (Glendenning, 2006: 332)

Leonard articulates grief in simple nouns: it comes into definition as a need to learn what a door or a window might, and might not, now signify in the impossibility of Virginia's return.

For Denise Riley, cliché is of interest because it represents a common vocabulary: 'its automatic comfort is the happy exteriority of a shared language which knows itself perfectly well to be a contentless but sociable turning outward toward the world' (2005: 4). In cliché, she explains, language is apprehended as an 'outward consciousness which hovers between people, rather than [as] swimming upward from the privacy of each heart' (2005: 4). Clichéd expression is not of our making; it conveys us or carries us along. Cliché marks the point at which the expression of individual feeling frays into what Ann Cvetkovich has described as a public 'archive of feelings' (2003: 7): it marks the confluence between personal sentiment and a more collective mode of feeling.

Riley's representation of cliché as a marker of our implication in the worlds of others might help to explain why the bereaved are propelled into cliché land. Judith Butler has remarked that mourning brings to the fore our relational ties, undoing our sense of ourselves as singular and coherent subjects:

> What grief displays ... is the thrall in which our relations with others hold us, in ways that we cannot always recount or explain, in ways that often interrupt the self-conscious account of ourselves we might try to provide, in ways that challenge the very notion of ourselves as autonomous and in control. I might try to tell a story here about what I am feeling, but it would have to be a story in which the very 'I' who

seeks to tell the story is stopped in the midst of the telling; the very
'I' is called into question by its relation to the Other, a relation that
does not precisely reduce me to speechlessness, but does nevertheless
clutter my speech with signs of its undoing. I tell a story about the
relations I choose, only to expose, somewhere along the way, the way
I am gripped and undone by these very relations. My narrative falters,
as it must.

(2004: 23)

Grief exposes how *I* is also composed of *you*, a state for which, Butler notes,
there is no 'ready vocabulary' (2004: 22). But perhaps cliché represents
exactly this vocabulary. If the thoughts of the bereaved so often revert to
cliché, is this then the expression of a subject for whom language has become
cluttered with the traces of her relation to others?

Riley's 'A Part Song', a poem sequence written after her son's death, enacts
cliché as at once undoing and sustaining the bereaved.[3] The poem is voiced
by a variety of speakers, in an attempt, as the mother confesses to her dead
son, 'to prod / And shepherd you back within range / Of my strained ears'
(2016: 14). Vikki Bell has described the poem as offering 'a sense of what
unravelling feels, or perhaps "sounds" like' (2020: 325). The voices notably
speak in the form of clichéd phrases and expressions. In *Time Lived*, Riley
noted her recurrent dread of losing another child: 'Now you expect another
death – a remaining child's – to be announced to you at any moment, and
you try to steady yourself for it' ([2012] 2019: 32). In 'A Part Song', this
anxiety surfaces in a cliché that comes unbidden into the speaker's mind.
As her daughter leaves the house: 'The thought rears up: *fix in your mind
this / Maybe final glimpse of her. Yes, lightning could*' (2016: 3). The thought
that – contrary to received wisdom – lightning could always strike in the
same place twice is cut short even as it is registered. The speaker's daughter,
too, might never return. Cliché carries the speaker's fear. It also conveys
that, although her feeling appears to 'rea[r] up' from within (2016: 3), it is
suspended between private grief and a more public form of utterance.

In the final part of the poem, the dead son finally speaks, and his words
comprise the closing voice of the sequence:

My sisters and my mother,
Weep dark tears for me
I drift as lightest ashes
Under a southern sea

O let me be, my mother
In no unquiet grave
My bone-dust is faint coral
Under the fretful wave.

(2016: 14)

For Sinéad Morrissey, these lines are freighted with the words of others: '[T]his utterance … carries echoes of both "Lycidas" ("he must not float upon his watery bier unwept") and Shakespeare's "Full Fathom Five" from *The Tempest* ("of his bones are coral made")' (2019: 22). The half echoes suggest to Morrissey that these words might be snatches of the voices of the dead; she accordingly notes that the writing of the poem seems to be less an act of 'original creation' and more a matter of 'tuning in' to the dead (2019: 23).

Many of the words in the closing lines of 'A Part Song' are nouns: tears, ashes, sea, mother, grave, coral, wave. Li's narrator observes that mothers become experts at catching – 'somersaulting spoons, half-eaten bananas and apples, half-ripe blood berries' (2019: 48). What, she asks Nikolai, can she catch now that he is dead? Nikolai responds: 'We will be catching each other's words, don't you see?' (2019: 48). That so many of the words caught by Li and Riley are clichés, or everyday turns of expression, is a reminder that, like catching a snatch of conversation, the articulation of grief emerges as an effect of linguistic circulation; our feelings are stitched together by what words we pick up and relay to others.

'She's really gone and done it now': my sister and I would say these words when we knew that one of us had gone too far. They signified that a line had been crossed; an act could no longer be undone. Sounding through my mind in the days after my sister's death, the phrase registered the gravity of what had happened, even as it softened the blow. It foreshadowed my realization of the reality of my sister's death, conveying me towards it as surely as the plane carried Handke towards his mother's body in Austria. The phrase hovered between me and my sister in death, as it had in life, representing that form of outward consciousness which Riley has so poignantly described.

It is here, too, perhaps, that Handke's sense of impersonal well-being might be parsed. The words which echo in Handke's thoughts constitute the fabric of his personal grief, but they do so precisely by coursing through him in an impersonal manner. Words are not in us, ready to obediently express our thoughts and desires, but move through, across and between us. Like the objects examined in Chapter 1, some words become sticky with association.

They form the phrases that we readily pick up and tune into. The clichéd thoughts of the bereaved represent, in Sara Ahmed's terms, how we 'feel our way' (2004: 12). They enable us to continue when we do not quite know how or what we feel or for whom. Their familiar and well-worn phrases reveal what sticks in the aftermath of sudden loss. In so doing, cliché provides a valuable, if often overlooked, resource for thinking with and through suicide.[4]

Pain scale

Li has remarked: 'A mother's job is to enfold, not to unfold' (2019: 5). What, then, is the role of the sister? Joanne Limburg lost her younger brother to suicide, and she takes up this question in her poem, 'Sister'.[5] The poem opens: 'She will harrow this town, she will turn him up, / whole or in pieces' (2017a: 10). Her part, we learn, is to 'rescue' her brother; if she cannot do that, then her task is 'to take him home, / and never mind how small the pieces' (2017a: 10). Enfolding here merges with, and is indissociable from, unfolding, as the poem's speaker searches tirelessly for her brother's remains.

In her memoir, *Small Pieces,* Limburg writes of attending a support day for Survivors of Bereavement by Suicide. The sibling group she joins is united by 'stories of police searches and dragged rivers, discussed … in the kind of detail you might expect from a forensic specialist' (2017b: 257). Limburg reflects that bereavement by suicide has turned the siblings 'into lay experts in areas we would never otherwise have thought, or wanted, to explore' (2017b: 257–8). Limburg's anecdote mirrors my own recollection of the time between my sister's death and the inquest four months later: not having been able to rescue my sister – to save her from drowning – my task became one of attending carefully to the details of her death. My need to know the facts about how my sister died was a way of 'keep[ing her] company' (Riley, [2012] 2019: 38) in death, because I had not been present at her dying.

The River Ouse was dragged for ten days after Virginia Woolf's disappearance, in the attempt to recover her body from the water. The search was then abandoned; it was most likely that Woolf's body had been carried out to sea by the strong tidal current of the river.[6] On 18 April 1941, five teenagers cycled out from Lewes to picnic by the river. Throwing stones at a log, to try to divert it from floating downriver on the tide, the boys discovered that the object in the river was Woolf's body. In Leonard's words, '[t]he horrible business of the identification' (Glendenning, 2006: 331) then took place at Newhaven mortuary. Leonard identified Virginia's body, even though it had been submerged in water for three weeks.[7]

I have always appreciated how fortunate we were that my sister's body had washed straight back onto the beach. We were thereby spared what Leonard described as the 'long-drawn-out horror' (Glendenning, 2006: 331) of the weeks between Woolf's death and the recovery of her body. By the time I learned of my sister's death, my parents had already identified her body at the mortuary. Her hair was still damp with seawater and had sand from the beach caught in it. She had not been in the water long enough for the condition of her body to deteriorate.

In the months after my sister's death, my focus was on whether her dying had been painful. Alison Wertheimer observes that it is a common response among those bereaved by suicide, who have not been present at the death, to want to know what the person has experienced, and she notes that 'being given information by other people about what is likely to have happened can help to lessen that preoccupation' (2014: 47). The problem with drowning, I quickly learned, is that it is subject to mythologization, and my initial investigations propelled me once again into cliché land. My sources were sharply divided as to whether drowning is agonizing or painless. Darran Anderson encountered the same problem when he researched the deaths of his paternal grandparents by drowning, each of whom disappeared into the waters of the River Foyle in Derry-Londonderry: 'They say the bodies of the drowned are found with torn muscles in their arms and shoulders, where they have been grasping out towards the light. Others say there is a serene sense of release, floating there, once the finite number of breaths in each life reaches zero' (2020: 188). Anderson could not ultimately say 'what it might be like to drown' (2020: 188). I was unable to reach such an agnostic position. Although I was repeatedly told that drowning does not hurt, I struggled to believe that this was true. How could the pressure of water on eyes, throat, lungs and stomach not be painful?

Apprehending the pain of others is a notoriously difficult matter, even when the subject is living.[8] In the case of the dead, there is only the body to rely on. After my parents had identified my sister, her body was held by the coroner until the post-mortem and preliminary inquest had been conducted. The coroner then issued a burial order, which meant that my sister's body could be released to the undertaker, which was where I caught up with her in the week following her death. Although I was advised not to view the body, I needed to do so in order to comprehend the reality of my sister's death. I also had lingering doubts about the state of her body after the drowning, despite my parents' reassurances. At the funeral home, the coffin was arranged so that only my sister's head was visible. Her face bore no sign of her passage through death. The residue of the beach that my parents had witnessed at the mortuary had been cleaned away. Everything had been carefully curated, and I did not stay in the viewing room for long. I wished that I, too, had viewed my sister's body at the mortuary.

Unless the body is immersed in water for an extended period, death by drowning leaves little visible trace on the surface of the body. It is typical of the suicide methods more commonly chosen by women. Wertheimer has observed of recent suicides in England and Wales:

> There are some significant differences in the methods men and women use to commit suicide. Women tend to opt for less violent methods and nearly half die as the result of self-poisoning or overdosing, compared with less than a quarter of male suicides. Forty-five per cent of males die by violent means such as hanging/suffocation, shooting, cutting/ stabbing or jumping/falling, whereas less than three out of ten female suicides use one of these methods.
>
> (2014: 6)

The method of suicide, and the degree to which it disfigures the body, has implications for the identification and/or viewing of the deceased. Sarah Manguso's memoir of her friend, Harris, who died by stepping out in front of a train, expresses uncertainty as to whether his parents identified the body or rather 'what was left of Harris's body' (13). She reflects: 'If I worked in a morgue, … I'd show the identifier a small part of [the body], whatever still resembled the outside of a body, or what the identifier might remember of the outside of it, if I could' (2012: 13). Manguso's phrasing recalls Limburg's 'small … pieces' (2017a: 10) and indicates that, when the body has been disfigured by death, it can still be important for relatives to have contact with what remains. My parents had been able to identify my sister's intact body, and I, too, could look at a face that was unchanged. Yet the body that I saw was not quite the same body that my parents had identified the previous week; the autopsy had intervened between my parents' encounter with my sister's body at the morgue and mine at the funeral home.

Following a suspected suicide, the coroner orders an autopsy to be performed. The post-mortem functions in the coronial process to establish the medical cause of death. It can also play an important role in determining whether the death has been intentionally self-inflicted, a requirement for the verdict of suicide to be reached. Depending on the mode of death, there may be a limited or a full post-mortem. The full autopsy involves a detailed examination of all the internal organs, including the brain, heart and lungs, which are removed, examined and then returned to the body. An incision is made down the front of the body and in the hair at the back of the head. Neither incision is visible once the body has been dressed and arranged for viewing.

My encounter with my sister's body after a full post-mortem had taken place was necessarily shaped by the procedure. I was aware that I could not see my sister's torso or the back of her head, both of which would have carried the sutured scars of a body dissected. Katrina Jaworski has noted that the autopsy is often more invasive when the method of suicide leaves less visible trace on the body's surface and so requires internal examination to establish the cause of death. The categorization of certain modes of death as less disfiguring than others is complicated, Jaworski observes, by bringing the post-mortem into consideration: '[T]he rendering of disfigurement is bound not only to those who engage with the act of suicide, but also to those who, as in the case of post-mortem examinations, either further disfigure or introduce disfigurement for the purpose of verifying suicide' (2014: 93). The autopsy is necessary to make the death both legible and intelligible, but it is an invasive procedure that can cause distress to the bereaved.

Although Denise Riley did not view her son's body, her account of reading his autopsy report captures the tension that I experienced between the knowledge of the death that the post-mortem could yield and the bodily harm inflicted in the process. Riley's son died of heart failure in the bath; for her, the autopsy report became critical in distinguishing whether the medical cause of death had been a heart attack or drowning. Riley became a lay expert in the physical signs of drowning as she sought to interpret the report: '[I]t demanded far more research into the nature of drowning, how you can distinguish death by water from death prior to immersion by the flooding of the lungs with small, haemorrhaged flecks of blood' ([2012] 2019: 37). The autopsy report satisfies Riley's need to know the facts about her son's death, yet she is left wondering about 'the degree of physical effort needed to shear open a chest. Or whether the ribs' cartilage is easily cut' ([2012] 2019: 37). The discrepancy between the specks of blood left on the lungs by drowning and the damage inflicted on the body in order to verify the evidence raises the question of how we read or interpret violence: drowning does not appear to be a violent death because the traces of that violence have been inscribed onto the interior organs of the body. The violence of the death is displaced onto the autopsy investigation, after the fact, because its marks are incised visibly into skin and bone.

For Jaworski, bodily disfigurement also comes to matter in how a suspected suicide is interpreted by the coroner. If a suicide method does not produce bodily disfigurement, if what it inscribes on the body 'appears bloodless', then, Jaworski contends, '[T]he lack of visible violence … is most likely to be seen as passive … with something else other than suicide in mind' (2014: 43). Intention is mapped onto the signs of external wounding through which self-infliction might be interpreted so that '[w]ounds, cuts and abrasions carry meanings' (2014: 93). The higher the degree of visible damage to the body, Jaworski opines, 'the more transparent, serious and *active* is the intent to die' (2014: 102). In cases of completed suicide that leave no visible markers on the body's surface, intentionality is often deemed to be either weak or lacking. Jaworski summarizes: '*[H]ow* the act of death is carried out shapes … *why* it has taken place. Suicidal intentions are rendered intelligible through a gendered reading of suicide methods' (2014: 102).

Central to Jaworski's argument is the idea that suicide is currently made sense of through binary pairings, 'male-female and masculine-feminine, but also completed-attempted and active-passive' (2014: 5). Read in the light of these pairings, it is evident that Woolf's representation of Septimus Smith's suicide in *Mrs. Dalloway*, through his leap from the window onto the railings below, is coded as masculine-completed-active. In contrast, overdosing – the most prevalent method of suicide chosen by women – is conceptualized as feminine-attempted-passive. Even when an overdose results in death, it is more likely to be perceived as a cry for help or attention gone awry, rather than a serious suicide attempt. Gender thus shapes which experiences of suicide are seen to be legitimate and valid. In Jaworski's eloquent phrasing, '[t]he fleshiness of bodies is crucial to [the production of suicide], etched with meanings already interpreted as gendered' (2014: 5).

My sister's death could not be named as suicide because the evidence of intentionality was weak. In Chapter 1, I noted that this was related to the imprecise time of her death, and it was also related to the lack of a suicide note. I cannot be certain whether *how* my sister died also shaped the understanding of motive when her death was interpreted in the coroner's court, but in leaving no visible traces on the surface of her body, drowning did not produce evidence of her intention. Self-infliction could not be mapped transparently onto my sister's lungs as it might be onto gun-shot wounds or marks left on the skin by a ligature. Stefan Timmermans has accordingly noted that, in cases of suspected suicide, '[d]rownings ... are equivocal and require further evidence to make the suicide classification stick' (2006: 87). The coroner could not ultimately rule out the possibility that my sister might have had something other than death in mind when she had entered the water on that late August day; consequently, an open verdict was returned.

Listening to the autopsy report as it was read out in the courtroom, my central concern was not with intentionality but with pain. Could the post-mortem help me to understand whether my sister's death by drowning had been painful? The lack of bodily disfigurement produced by drowning might account for the widespread belief that it is a painless way to die. Drowning is also a silent mode of dying: the instinctive drowning response prevents cries for help, as the arms involuntarily press down on the water to raise the mouth above its surface in order to take in air. When seawater flooded into my sister's lungs, I learned that she would have experienced intense and severe chest pain. She would have lost consciousness after several minutes, followed closely by cardiac arrest and death.

In 'The Pain Scale', Eula Biss asks how we can effectively measure pain. Her essay is structured according to the numerical scale of zero to ten, which is commonly used to assess pain in clinical contexts. Biss explains that the medical pain scale comprises 'a simple number line complicated only by two phrases. Under zero: "no pain". Under ten: "the worst pain imaginable"' (2012: 11). Zero is a mathematical necessity, giving the scale a fixed point, but Biss questions the possibility – and the desirability – of experiencing no pain, which is a sign of vitality itself: 'Does the absence of pain equal the absence of everything?' (2012: 5).

Striving to conceive what ten, 'the worst pain imaginable', might feel like, Biss considers whether a more effective pain scale might rate 'what patients would be willing to do to relieve their pain' (2012: 24). Reading statements gathered by the American Pain Foundation, which advocates on behalf of people experiencing chronic or intractable pain, Biss becomes 'alarmed by the number of references to suicide' (2012: 24). In measuring pain, its duration as well as its intensity must surely be taken into consideration. Biss calls attention to the severe mental-health symptoms that can be caused by chronic or incurable pain, and that are not sufficiently recognized. The pain of mental illness can be equally devastating and even more difficult to quantify or evidence. Biss makes us aware of the varieties of pain – physical, mental, emotional, spiritual or financial – that can underlie the suicidal act. By what scale, she asks, do we measure the pain for which death is sought as a relief?

The equivalent of ten on the Beaufort Scale – used for the measurement of wind – carries the descriptor, 'devastation occurs', which, Biss observes, '[b]rings us ... back to zero' (2012: 25). Biss's words recall Anderson's evocation of drowning as a 'sense of release, floating there, once the finite number of breaths in each life reaches zero' (2012: 188). Gathering the pieces and fragments I have gleaned about my sister's death I believe that, in her last moments of consciousness, my sister's pain could have approached the point of devastation. I cling to the hope that my sister's passage from ten back to zero – the point of no pain – was mercifully swift and to the assurance that, in reaching zero, my sister found the release from pain, as well as from life itself, that she had been seeking.

Affective atmospheres

Suicide, as the word is commonly used, refers to a completed act, while *suicidal* designates the thought, feeling or impulse that underpins the act and that constitutes evidence of an intention to die. Both these words are relatively recent in everyday usage. Suicide gradually began to replace self-murder prior to the nineteenth century, although not in any systematic or straightforward way. The evolving science of statistics enabled suicide to emerge as a discrete object of study throughout Europe in the nineteenth century, as the figures from coroners' courts were mapped onto populations. Asa Jansson remarks that the linguistic shift reflected a cultural turn from self-murder as a criminal act towards suicide as having origins in social causes: '[S]ocial environment became central to the perceived incidence of self-accomplished deaths within a nation or group of people, ... which culminated in [Émile] Durkheim's famous 1897 study [*Suicide: A Study in Sociology*]' (2013: 717).

In 1824, the Burial of Suicides Act suspended the prohibition on burying the body in consecrated ground following a coronial verdict of suicide. However, it was not until the passing of the Suicide Act in 1961 that suicide and attempted suicide were finally decriminalized in England.[9] Even then, Lucy Biddle observes, the coroners' courts 'continue[d] to implicitly process suicide as if it were a crime' (2003: 1043), meaning that the suicide inquest has come to represent a procedural anachronism:

Unlike other inquests which may directly result in legislative change or preventative public health measures, it is more difficult to arrive at a modern-day purpose for the suicide inquest. Indeed, the suicide inquest seems to have more to do with tradition than functional necessity since its origins relate to when suicide was a crime and the property of those committing this offence was forfeited to the crown. The public inquest was essentially a criminal trial for this purpose. ... The suicide case is therefore a 'misfit' that presents today's coroner with something of a contradiction in practice since it still hinges around establishing intent and attaching a moral classification to the cause of death.

(2003: 1033–4)

I return to the idea of the contemporary suicide inquest as an outdated phenomenon at the close of this chapter. For now, it is worth noting that some coroner's verdicts can support legal and social reform: China Mills cites the ruling on the disabled Michael O'Sullivan's death by hanging in 2014 as 'a direct result of being ruled "fit to work"', as marking 'the first official link of W[ork] C[apability] A[ssessments] to suicide' (2020: 80).[10] In requiring deaths by suicide to be registered, the coroner's court has also provided what Chris Millard has described as an 'organised and systematic ... source' (2015: 28) of information for those who study, analyse or interpret the incidence of deaths by suicide.

The adjective 'suicidal' was used alongside the noun 'suicide' during the nineteenth century, but Millard notes that there was 'no easy relationship' (2015: 28) between the two terms. Suicidal emerged as a medical rather than a legal concept: the increasing prevalence of the category reflected a growing belief that suicide was explicable. Jansson outlines that a new medical approach to suicide 'made the potential "signs" that a person might be contemplating self-destruction a legitimate, indeed a valuable, object of study' (2013: 717). The term 'suicidal' made its first appearance in the medical certificates of insanity that were introduced in the first decades of the nineteenth century. As part of the process of registration into an asylum, the reception order accompanying the medical certificate required a statement of whether the patient was considered suicidal. Jansson explains that the category was 'transferred from reception orders and onto the pages of patient case books', which were used to produce 'tables displaying the number of patients with "suicidal propensities" residing in the asylum at any one time' (2013: 717). Millard traces the registration of suicidal intentionality – in the form of a suicide attempt – into the twentieth century, when it was first recorded by 'general hospital A[ccident] & E[mergency] departments' and then by 'psychiatric inpatient facilities' (2015: 29). Data about suicidal populations was gathered separately from suicide statistics and was less readily accessible than the information collected by the coroner's office. It was more straightforward, Millard contends, to 'catalogue the dead' than to record 'the living attempter' (2015: 28).

Charles Dickens's *Bleak House* is celebrated for its attack on the Court of Chancery, which presided over disputes relating to wills, trusts and estates. By the mid-nineteenth century, Chancery was renowned for its lengthy and opaque proceedings, and Dickens produces a barely exaggerated version in the case of Jarndyce & Jarndyce. From the very first pages of Dickens's novel, Chancery has a clear causal connection to suicide in the person of old Tom Jarndyce, who 'in despair blew his brains out at a coffee-house in Chancery-lane' (Dickens 2008: 14). Coronial law is also referred to in *Bleak House*: the coroner summons inquests at the Sol's Arms to investigate two unusual deaths, each of which takes place at the grimy rag-and-bottle shop belonging to Mr. Krook – the first is that of Nemo, whom we later identify as Captain Hawdon, and the second is that of Krook. Both men are fatally entangled with Lady Dedlock: she had an affair with Hawdon in her youth and subsequently gave birth to Esther, while Mr. Guppy and Mr. Weevle discover the remains of Krook when they search his rooms for stolen papers that would expose Lady Dedlock's secret. Suicide haunts these deaths, as well as the death of Lady Dedlock herself, with which the novel culminates. In what follows, I consider suicide and coronial law in *Bleak House*, arguing that the relation between the two is an altogether stickier business than the straightforward, causal relation that Dickens establishes between suicide and Chancery.

Caroline Levine has influentially analysed *Bleak House* as a 'complex heaping of networks that not only stretch across space but also unfold over time' (2015: 115). Using the expansive narrative frame afforded by the multiplot novel, Dickens created a series of intersecting networks that enabled him to connect apparently disparate lives. The 'most obvious principle of interconnection', Levine explains, is 'the lawsuit of Jarndyce & Jarndyce' (2015: 123), but she also itemizes a range of other devices through which the novel's characters are linked: these include the city, as London is portrayed as a dense tangle of streets that radiate out from the Court of Chancery; kinship, which links Lady Dedlock to Nemo and to Esther through the former's secret affair; and disease, as smallpox passes from one character to another, connecting together very different social groups and spaces.

Coronial law can also be understood as a network in *Bleak House*, which intersects with a variety of other networks. The coroner's formal investigations into the deaths of Nemo and Krook overlap with Inspector Bucket's subsequent police investigation into the disappearance of Lady Dedlock, linking the inquest proceedings to detective work through a common interest in motive and intention. Coronial law is related to the Chancery case of Jarndyce & Jarndyce, but it is distinct in its exclusive concern with the elucidation of unexplained deaths. Levine observes of Dickens's intricately networked novel: '[W]hat is perhaps most strange and compelling … is that this sublime complexity captures something all too ordinary at work. All of us, along with other species and objects, are located at the crossings of multiple unfolding networks that are perpetually linking bodies, ideas, and things' (2015: 130). The coronial process in *Bleak House* represents the meeting point of multiple agencies, although it is notable that, in their mutual entanglement, suicide repeatedly fails to materialize as verdict.

Nemo's body is discovered in his rented room at the rag-and-bottle shop by his landlord, Krook, and the lawyer, Mr. Tulkinghorn, who was seeking to employ Nemo 'at his trade of copying' (2008: 154). The surgeon is summoned, and the medical cause of death is immediately established to be 'an over-dose of opium' (2008: 153). The question of intention is less transparent: the surgeon muses that it is 'unlikely' that Nemo has died on purpose, 'as he has been in the habit of taking so much [opium]' – although, he adds, 'nobody can tell' (2008: 154). The inquest into Nemo's death takes place the following day, opening with the formal viewing of the body in the rented room at Mr. Krook's, 'from which a few of the Jurymen retire pale and precipitately' (2008: 160). In nineteenth-century England, an inquest almost always included a viewing of the body: Jaworski notes that suicide was legally recognized 'through physically sustained visible markings that confirmed and conformed to what was interpreted as violence' (2014: 65). Nemo's overdose has left no marks of violence on his body, and, as the inquiry proceeds, no facts can be established other than how Nemo died and that he was in the habit of taking large quantities of opium. Not even a proper name can be assigned to the body – Nemo, the name by which Captain Hawdon is known to those present at the inquest, designates 'no-one' in Latin – and the verdict of 'Accidental Death' (2008: 162) is accordingly returned. Nemo's body represents a surface onto which nothing, including the verdict of suicide, can be made to stick.

The word 'suicidal' appears in *Bleak House* in reference to the room in which Nemo died. Mr. Weevle, who is Krook's replacement tenant in the room, observes to Mr. Guppy of his mood: 'I am in the Downs. It's this unbearably dull, suicidal room – and old Boguey [Krook] down-stairs, I suppose' (2008: 469–70). Suicidal feeling is accorded to the room: the death that has taken place there seems to have permeated its walls and fabric, just as fog emanates from the High Court of Chancery to hang over London in the novel's famous opening paragraphs. Or perhaps the atmosphere of the room itself, which is reflected in the 'tainting sort of weather' (2008: 467) on the night Weevle and Guppy meet there, has been the cause of Nemo's demise. Diana Rose Newby has observed 'the active role that atmosphere plays throughout [*Bleak House*], both surrounding and significantly shaping the human characters' lives' (2020: 183). A suicidal aura hovers over Krook's lodgings, forming what Newby has described as a 'weathering influenc[e]' (2020: 180) on those who reside within.

The second inquest in *Bleak House* investigates the death of Krook after what remains of him has been discovered by Weevle and Guppy. Krook's charred remains, following his death by spontaneous combustion, are the source of a malignant miasma that emanates from his room. Krook has become a substance that sticks: he has dissolved into the 'stagnant, sickening oil' (2008: 476) which coats Guppy's fingers and that cannot be washed away. At the inquest, Mr. Swills testifies to 'the impure state of the atmosphere' (2008: 480) on the night of Krook's death, and Mrs. Piper and Mrs. Perkins witnessed a 'foetid effluvia … being emitted from the premises' (2008: 481). Krook's combustion into soot and grease means he has become indissociable from what Matthew Beaumont has termed 'those less spontaneous modes of combustion associated with the processes of industrial production' (2012: 817). What, in the end, constitutes Krook, and what the sooty London atmosphere, cannot be distinguished, leading Newby to claim that in *Bleak House*, 'Dickens gives hazy shape to a new way of knowing: atmospherically' (2020: 199).

Anna Harpin has noted that atmospheres, like the fog in *Bleak House*, are not singular or fixed but 'diffuse' and 'relational' (2018: 208). For Tim Ingold, atmospheres arise from 'the coming together of persons and things' (2015: 77): although they seem to exist out there, beyond us, atmospheres constitute the very medium in which we live. We experience the quality of the atmosphere as weather; thus, Krook's death is signified as a meteorological phenomenon, a localized weather front that hangs over the rag-and-bottle shop. Newby indicates that Krook's spontaneous combustion 'exaggerates in order to make more obvious the impact of weather on individual bodies' (2020: 196). Occurring instantaneously, Krook's demise shows the effect of exposure to a tainting atmosphere without the extended duration that weathering typically implies.

When Lady Dedlock disappears, Inspector Bucket observes to her husband, Sir Leicester Dedlock, 'it looks like suicide. Anyways there's more and more danger, every minute, of its drawing to that' (2008: 797). Lady Dedlock's past has closed in on her, in the form of Mr. Tulkinghorn, who has uncovered her secret and intends to expose her affair to her husband. Speaking with Lady Dedlock at Sir Leicester's ancestral seat of Chesney Wold in Lincolnshire – notable throughout the novel for its rainy weather and damp atmosphere – Tulkinghorn watches Lady Dedlock closely for any sign of suicidal intention:

> His jealous glance as she walks [to the window] betrays an instant's misgiving that she may have it in her thoughts to leap over, and dashing against a ledge and cornice, strike her life out upon the terrace below. But, a moment's observation of her figure as she stands in the window without any support, looking out at the stars – not up – gloomily out at those stars which are low in the heavens – reassures him.
>
> (2008: 607)

The death that Tulkinghorn momentarily envisages for Lady Dedlock will be realized by Septimus Smith in *Mrs. Dalloway*, in his plunge from the window of his Bloomsbury lodging house. Bucket has in mind an altogether different death, as his search for Lady Dedlock takes him and Esther to Limehouse, where the bodies of the drowned were brought out for identification and burial. Bucket examines a body that has been washed ashore, but it is not that of Lady Dedlock, while Esther watches the 'tide ... coming in' and 'shudder[s]' (2008: 804) at the thought that it might carry her mother's body on to the shore of the River Thames. Returning to the binary pairings through which suicide is constructed, Lady Dedlock's projected suicide by drowning is coded as feminine and passive; it is not the active leap from the window that Tulkinghorn had earlier dismissed from his thoughts.

Lady Dedlock's departure from Chesney Wold is described as a dissipation into the atmosphere, as she 'flutters away, in the shrill frosty wind' (2008: 791). When her body is discovered by Esther, Lady Dedlock's death is closer to the watery end anticipated by Bucket: lying on the threshold of Hawdon's pauper's grave, Lady Dedlock is 'drenched in the fearful wet of such a place, which oozed and splashed down everywhere' (2008: 844). Her saturated body resembles the drowned body that Esther had feared would be washed ashore on the tide. For Newby, the imagery of flooding prevalent in Lady Dedlock's death scene provides 'a fitting symbol for the tide of cultural forces that erode her foothold in society' and 'engul[f] … her agency' (2020: 189). Once again, the female body is rendered passive in the face of the elements to which it is exposed. Read atmospherically, however, Lady Dedlock's death offers, in Newby's terms, 'a figure for the environment's very real power over the individual' (2020: 189). That Lady Dedlock's intention, in exposing herself to the storm, is too weak to be designated suicidal is arguably the point: Dickens relates a different story of suicide, which is based not on individual motive but is connected to social and environmental influence.

Richard Carstone, an orphan and ward of Chancery taken into Bleak House by John Jarndyce, enters the legal profession and becomes consumed by the case of Jarndyce & Jarndyce. His death, seemingly from exhaustion, is causally linked to the Chancery case, although it cannot be designated as suicide in the straightforward manner of old Tom Jarndyce. Observing Richard's growing obsession with the Jarndyce case, Mr. Weevle observes to Mr. Guppy: '[T]here's combustion going on there! It's not a case of Spontaneous, but it's smouldering combustion it is' (2008: 583). Smouldering combustion aptly describes the deaths of Captain Hawdon and Lady Dedlock, as well as of Richard. It captures the gradual, weathering effects of the hostile environments to which all these characters are exposed, and which wear them down to the point that their lives do not end, so much as disperse into the noxious atmospheres in which they are immersed. Hawdon's exposure is to poverty, and his body becomes absorbed into the 'impure … atmosphere' (2008: 480) of Krook's lodging house and the pauper's graveyard. Lady Dedlock is exposed to the double standards of the aristocracy, signified in the creeping damp of Chesney Wold, to which she eventually succumbs in her watery demise. Dickens points to a new way of relating suicide that registers the slow, seeping effects of environmental harms. Weather gives Dickens a way of describing their influence, as well as of illustrating that bodies absorb and are susceptible to their environments in smouldering, as well as in spontaneous, processes of combustion.

Coronial law in *Bleak House* intersects with a further network identified by Levine, namely 'rumour' (2015: 123). Even as Krook and Tulkinghorn leave Nemo's room on the night of his death, 'the news has got into the court' and 'the outposts of the army of observation … are pushed forward to Mr. Krook's window, which they closely invest' (2008: 157). On the day of Nemo's inquest, the Sol's Arms is 'like a fair' and 'does a brisk stroke of business all the morning' (2008: 159). At the Harmonic Meeting in the pub that evening, the proceedings are replayed by Mr. Swills 'with recreative intervals of piano-forte accompaniment' (2008: 164). Like Clarissa's party in *Mrs. Dalloway*, the inquest in Dickens's novel comprises a social gathering at which the news of the death is related. If the legal paraphernalia of the inquest already seems outmoded in *Bleak House* – the beadle, for example, is viewed by the policeman as 'something that must be borne with until Government shall abolish him' (2008: 158) – its purpose seems to lie rather in providing a space in which rumour can be given shape and definition, condensing an atmosphere into a finding. The inquest is a hearing that listens to the various assembled witnesses, and it absorbs a mysterious death into the everyday business and routine of the public house.

Biddle observes that the most prominent themes to emerge from families regarding contemporary inquest proceedings are feelings of 'stigma and criminalisation' (2003: 1036). Many relatives, she observes, feel in the inquest that 'they and the deceased [are] being publicly judged and condemned ... thereby adding to the shame and stigma already felt due to the nature of their bereavement' (2003: 1036). Sara Ahmed has described shame as an inherently social emotion, noting that 'shame is about appearance, about how the subject appears before and to others' (2004: 104–5). She remarks of shame's inward propulsion:

> Shame ... involves an impulse to 'take cover' and 'to cover oneself'. But the desire to take cover and to be covered presupposes the failure of cover; in shame, one desires cover precisely because one has already been exposed to others. ... On the one hand, shame covers that which is exposed (we turn away, we lower our face, we avert our gaze), while on the other, shame exposes that which has been covered (it un-covers). Shame in exposing that which has been covered demands us to re-cover; such a re-covering would be a recovery from shame.
>
> (2004: 104)

Reading Ahmed's words in the context of suicide, the death is often experienced by families as an initial moment of exposure. Attempts to take cover are undone by the inquest, which exposes once again that which is in the process of being covered. The public nature of the inquest means that the bereaved are unable to turn away from the gaze of others. If the recovery from shame entails a re-covering, then the inquest tends in the opposite direction.

For Biddle, the formality of the inquest carries associations of the criminal trial, including 'the court appearance … ; the terminology – giving evidence and reaching a verdict; and the required conduct such as swearing oaths over the Bible' (2003: 1036). Wertheimer concurs, noting that '[t]he whole process … has a strongly legal flavour, with the paraphernalia of statements, evidence, summonsing and cross-examination of witnesses, verdicts, and, in certain cases, the presence of a jury' (2014: 80). The circumstances surrounding the death are a matter of public investigation and statements from the family are supplemented by accounts from other witnesses, such as the person who discovered the body and the attending police officer. Additional evidence might include suicide notes, the pathologist's autopsy report, and medical or psychiatric records. In England and Wales, the media is also routinely present at the inquest: Wertheimer points out that the '[r]eporting of suicides in local newspapers is common practice' (2014: 87). In Scotland, the inquest is not public in nature: Alison Chapple et al. indicate that verdicts are determined 'in private on the basis of medical reports and opinion and other information' (2012: 237). The media presence at the inquest, and the subsequent reporting of the case, can increase a sense of shame, leaving the family feeling even more exposed to the public gaze.

I was not summoned as a witness at my sister's inquest because I had not been present on the day of her death. My parents were questioned by the coroner regarding my sister's movements on the morning of that day and were asked to confirm the events leading to their identification of her body in the early hours of the following morning. I learned from the man who discovered my sister's body that she had been floating face-down in the shallow water, and I realized that I had inadvertently conjured up a clichéd image of her as Ophelia, floating on her back. From the police statement, I discovered exactly where my sister had been washed onto the beach: her body was in front of two waste pipes that drain onto the Stray, at the point where the groynes give way to the open sands. The inquest helped me to piece together more of what had happened, and I found it helpful to see, and to hear from, those who had attended my sister's body in the hours immediately following her death. I found more difficult those aspects of the inquest in which the coroner addressed the question of intention. Biddle has noted that a common response of the bereaved is a sense of losing 'all control over the interpretation given to … information' (2003: 1036). Her observation chimes with my own experience: the inquest enabled my sister's death to be publicly related, but it also placed the narrative authority for defining what the story would be outside the family.

My encounter with the coroner's court revealed that stigmatization has marked the contemporary inquest not only procedurally but at a more structural level. Under coronial law in England and Wales, the verdict on my sister's death had to conform to the criminal, rather than to the civil, standard of evidence; that is, it had to be proven beyond reasonable doubt, not considered according to the balance of probabilities. The criminal standard of evidence in coronial proceedings can be traced back to the criminalization of suicide, and it continued to be used even after the Suicide Act of 1961. In May 2019, the Court of Appeal in England and Wales handed down a ruling that upheld a decision taken at the High Court in 2018 that the standard of proof required to reach a suicide verdict should be the civil standard. This followed a campaign for the adoption of the civil standard of evidence by suicide-prevention charities, which were, as Pauline Turnbull et al. have noted, concerned about 'the underestimation [of deaths by suicide] that a higher standard [of evidence] makes inevitable' (2019: no pagination). I do not know whether a different verdict would have been reached had my sister's death been considered according to the civil standard of evidence, but it would have been almost impossible to have received a suicide verdict under the criminal standard, given the method that my sister chose and the absence of a suicide note.

Chapple et al. have observed that 'the UK is one of the countries with the highest proportion of undetermined deaths (open verdicts)' (2012: 231). The official policy in England and Wales, adopted by the National Office for Statistics in 2006, has accordingly been, they note, to define as suicide 'all deaths where the coroner has given a verdict of suicide or open verdict' (2012: 231) – a measure that was brought in to tackle the problem of under-recording. With the introduction of the civil standard, the overall number of deaths classified as suicide may therefore not see as sharp a rise as might be predicted. Turnbull et al. argue, rather, that the change will be evident at a more granular level, making visible those suicides that were more likely to be returned as an open verdict under the higher standard of evidence: 'Uncertainty over a person's intent is often the reason a death does not meet the criminal standard. Any rise may therefore be greater in groups whose suicidal intent can be harder to ascertain – for example, young people or those who died from self-poisoning, which is more often associated with women' (2019: no pagination). The new figures are likely to produce a shift in the demographic spread of suicide across the population. For suicide prevention charities, the civil standard of proof should, according to Turnbull et al., 'give a more accurate picture' and 'bring higher political priority' (2019: no pagination).

Whichever standard of evidence is applied, the coronial court relates a single narrative of suicide: it is exclusively concerned with individual intention. My reading of *Bleak House* has indicated an alternative, 'atmospheric', mode of relating suicide, which connects it to social and environmental influences that act gradually and invisibly on the individual in slow processes of attrition. Questions of agency, as well as of intention, are at stake here. Katrina Jaworski has noted that, in the coronial process, '[t]he individual is assumed to be the origin of the intention to die' (2010: 677). Invoking Judith Butler's theory of performativity, Jaworski reads suicide, rather, as 'a reiterative and citational practice, made possible through norms, meanings, assumptions, and knowledges identified within existing historical conditions and patterns' (2010: 680). Thus, suicide methods change over time and across place, indicating that 'suicide has a discursive history' (2010: 680). Agency does not disappear in this model of suicide, Jaworski notes, but it does accrue 'a layered history on which the deliberateness in the taking depends' (2010: 681). My emphasis has been less on suicide's relation to prior suicides than on broader social and economic factors, but here, too, Jaworski's unsettling of agency is apposite: '[S]uicide', she observes, 'is not simply *done* in the moment of its articulation, because a chain of effects and affects are in circulation already' (2020: 594). To look at broader social factors in the context of suicide is not simply to transfer agency from the individual to her environment but rather to recognize, in Jaworski's terms, that there are 'contexts that … shape … each act of suicide' (2020: 594). Atmosphere enables us to articulate something of suicide's more diffuse and distributed agency, which entails that the individual person is not attributed as the 'sole owner' of her act (2020: 594).

The question of violence and its (in)visibility is also relevant here. Rob Nixon has observed, in terms that can be applied to the suicidal act, that violence is 'customarily conceived as an event or action that is immediate in time, explosive and spectacular in space, and as erupting into instant sensational visibility' (2013: 2). Contrary to such dramatic instances of violence, Nixon's concern is with the 'incremental and accretive' (2013: 2) violence of environmental harms; he shifts our attention from an acute to a chronic temporality. His 'slow violence' (2013: 2) is analogous to the smouldering combustion through which Dickens conveys the delayed and dispersed effects of social affliction. A key challenge, Nixon has contended, is 'how we can convert into narrative … disasters that are slow moving and long in the making' (2013: 3). In the context of suicide, how might we make more visible the social and environmental factors that can contribute to suicidal behaviours? How can we, in the terms offered by Jasbir K. Puar, '"slow" the act of suicide down', which is also to ask, 'what kinds of "slow deaths" have been ongoing that a suicide might represent an escape from?' (2011: 152). I begin the following chapter by exploring what forms of relating suicide might capture the 'long dying' (Nixon, 2013: 2) which can result from a sustained erosion of life-sustaining conditions and environments, as well as the event of the death.

Notes

1   Published as fiction, *Where Reasons End* was written in the months after Li's son ended his life, aged sixteen. At the time of her son's death, Li had been writing a novel in which a mother loses her child to suicide when she is forty-four – Li's age when her son died. Li refers to returning to this novel at the end of *Where Reasons End* (2019: 169), and it was subsequently published as *Must I Go* (2020).

2   Szirtes's mother was imprisoned in the concentration camp at Büchenwald in central Germany. Although he does not attribute a cause-and-effect relationship between his mother's persecution in the Holocaust and her suicide, Szirtes's book, read alongside Adorján's memoir of her grandparents, who were also survivors of the Nazi persecution, calls attention to the intergenerational effects of genocide and persecution on survivors' families.

3   'A Part Song' was first published in *The London Review of Books* in 2012 and was awarded the Forward Prize for Best Poem in that year. It was subsequently included in *Say Something Back* (2016); my quotations from the poem refer to this collection.

4   Andrew Bennett has notably discussed cliché's relation to suicide in his reading of James Joyce's work (2017: 72–107).

5   'Sister' is the first poem in Limburg's elegy for her brother, *Oxygen Man* (2012). I refer to its re-publication in *The Autistic Alice* (2017).

6   Victoria Glendenning records that Vanessa Bell and Vita Sackville-West were both 'relieved' that Woolf's body had not been found, taking comfort from the idea of her being swept out into the sea she had loved so much (2006: 330).

7   Anu Salmela is interested in how non-human agencies interact with the body to affect the autopsy process, noting in the context of nineteenth-century Finnish post-mortems that the weather could 'accelerat[e] [the] decomposition' of the body (2018: 15). In cases of drowning, water might be viewed as a comparable agent in the production of suicide because of its equivalent effect of speeding up the temporality of decay if immersion is prolonged.

8   Elaine Scarry influentially declared pain's 'resistance to language', which means that it 'comes unsharably into our midst as at once that which cannot be denied

and that which cannot be confirmed' (1985: 4). Joanna Bourke has challenged this position, arguing that pain 'changes over time' and is 'constructed by a host of discourses, including theological, clinical, and psychological ones' (2014: 3). For Bourke, pain is inherently social, and it is experienced differently over time and across place, according to the metaphors and language with which we understand it.

9   Wertheimer points out that, even as the Suicide Act of 1961 decriminalized the act of suicide, it 'introduced a new criminal offence: aiding, abetting, counselling or procuring the suicide of another person carries the penalty of up to fourteen years' imprisonment' (2014: 13).

10 Margrit Shildrick has further noted of the link between Work Capability Assessment and suicide in the UK: '[D]isability activist [Merry] Cross (2013) … highlights one of the most pernicious outcomes of the WCA in her claim that in 2011 there were at least thirty suicides resulting from punitive assessments. The latest official figures released by the Department of Work and Pensions in late 2014 point to sixty more benefit-related suicides in the subsequent two years' (2015: 18).

Figure 4 Tide clock, 2021. Photograph © the author

3
WHERE?

A cracked barometer

In my photograph of the Stray with which this book begins (Figure 1), we are looking out to the sea into which my sister walked. The line of wooden posts leads our eye inexorably to the vanishing point of the horizon. This section asks what comes into view if we shift our gaze and turn in a different direction. Instead of looking out over the water, let's consider what lies behind and around us. Refocusing our attention in this way enables us to come at the question that sets this chapter in motion: how do we connect suicide and place? Avril Maddrell has observed that the relation between death and place 'has long been an important preoccupation of epidemiologists and social scientists with demographers and health geographers mapping varying rates of ... mortality between ... and within countries' (2015: 169). I accordingly begin by looking at how social scientists have described the relation between suicide and place and then ask how two writers of contemporary memoirs have mapped suicide onto their own place of Derry-Londonderry, which has experienced escalating suicide rates, particularly among the young, since the signing of the Good Friday Agreement in 1998. The second section of this chapter turns its gaze onto practices of vernacular memorialization. I consider vernacular memorials as meaningful materializations of grief, which can help both the bereaved and the dead to be integrated back into the community after a suicide. I close by asking what kind of journey grief comprises, considering its relational aspect. How does suicide bring people together – in a physical or a virtual space – and might we think of suicide, in Jocelyn Lim Chua's terms, not simply as 'terminating life' but as generating ways 'to live differently and to live differently with one another' (2014: 5)?

I took the photograph on the Stray in August 2019. Out of frame behind me, and a little to my left, was the decaying hulk of the blast furnace of Redcar steel works, the second largest operating in Europe at the time of its closure in 2015. The furnace was still active when my sister died in 1998: having survived the privatization of British Steel in the 1990s, it would limp through a series of international investors before the furnace was finally cooled completely and steel-making ended on the site. Jonathan Warren observed that, alongside the redundancies, the closure of the steelworks 'shattered the social relationships that underpinned the … fabric of the lives of those living and working on Teesside' (2018: 41). As the steel industry was replaced by precarious working conditions and zero-hour contracts, the prevailing atmosphere on Teesside became, Warren notes, one of 'insecurity and a feeling of being left on the margins' (2018: 41). In 2018, Middlesbrough became the suicide capital of the UK with a suicide rate over 70 per cent higher than the national average. To my right, as I took the photograph, was Hunt Cliff, which rises sheer above the former fishing village of Saltburn-by-the-Sea. There were so many suicides at Hunt Cliff that, a few weeks after my visit and to mark World Suicide Prevention Day, the National Trust erected a suicide prevention sign at the base of the cliff. The Samaritans' sign accompanies the existing signage at the peak of the cliff in a bid to reduce the number of fatalities at the site. Looking at what was not captured by my camera's lens on that August day turns a place that holds a personal association with suicide into a broader geography of despair. How do we relate suicide to a place that has been left behind? In Rob Nixon's terms, how might we narrate the 'slow violence' (2013: 2) of sustained socio-economic erosion?

Social scientists and health geographers have mapped the relation between suicide and areas of social and economic deprivation, and their research affords a helpful starting point for considering these questions. Working against the prevailing tendency to map suicide onto adverse individual circumstances, Danny Dorling and David Gunnell questioned whether the place where people lived influenced suicidal behaviour. They found that areas of high unemployment in the UK also tended to experience high rates of suicide, leading Dorling and Gunnell to observe that 'the economic geography of the changing availability of work has had a significant impact on the suicide rate in different places' (2003: 443). Nevertheless, they caution that living in an area where being out of work is common has a stronger influence on suicide among men than women, noting: '[w]ho you are matters as much as where you live … in terms of your [suicide] risk' (2003: 443).

In a Samaritans report on the relation between socio-economic disadvantage and suicidal behaviour, Clare Bambra and Joanne Cairns confirmed 'strong evidence' of an association between suicide risk and area-level deprivation in the UK (2017: 25), arguing: 'it is important to think about both people *and* places' (2017: 26). They recorded significant differences in suicide rates across the different countries of the UK with Scotland experiencing the highest suicide rate, followed by Northern Ireland, Wales and then England. There were also notable variations within each of the countries. In England, 'local authorities in more urban areas and those in the North exhibi[ted] higher suicide rates than those in rural areas, although with some exceptions, e.g. coastal areas such as Cornwall and Devon in the South West' (2017: 10). In Northern Ireland, suicide rates 'were higher in more deprived areas' (2017: 19). Although Wales and Northern Ireland had recognized area-level deprivation 'as an important factor for suicide risk' (2017: 25), Bambra and Cairns noted that England and Scotland had yet to follow suit.

Bambra and Cairns observe that social scientists have recourse to two narrative strategies for mapping suicide onto place: the compositional and the contextual. According to the compositional explanation, 'it is "*who you are*" that matters for health' (2017: 21). The health of a given area is 'a result of the different characteristics of the people who live the[re]' (2017: 20). In the context of suicide, the compositional approach would, Bambra and Cairns point out, emphasize factors such as 'accumulated adverse life course experiences (e.g., health, employment, living conditions); powerlessness, stigma and disrespect; experiencing other features of social exclusion (e.g., poverty, poor educational attainment); poor physical and mental health; unhealthy lifestyles; and social disconnectedness (e.g., loneliness, social isolation, poor social support, negative relationships)' (2017: 21).

The contextual explanation, on the other hand, 'suggests that "*where you live*" … contributes to area-level health: poor places lead to poor health' (2017: 21). This approach would, according to Bambra and Cairns, focus on the following considerations when looking at suicide: 'physical (e.g., poor housing conditions); cultural (e.g., tolerant attitudes to suicide); political (e.g., adverse public policy); economic (e.g., weak social capital); history (e.g., high incidence of suicidal behaviour); infrastructure (e.g., poor quality, accessibility, acceptability of services); and health and wellbeing (e.g., high prevalence of poor general and mental health)' (2017: 22–3). Bambra and Cairns point out that it is important to see these two frameworks not as separate or competing but as 'interact[ing] and shap[ing] one another' (2017: 23). For my purposes, these intersecting narratives offer a lens through which to approach two memoirs by writers who have each related suicide to their hometown of Derry-Londonderry: Darran Anderson's *Inventory* and Kerri ní Dochartaigh's *Thin Places*.

The first suicide in Anderson's memoir is that of his cousin DD, who was a few years older than Anderson and worked in a technology firm on an industrial estate at the edge of the city. Early one morning, his brother bumped into DD as he made his way back from a night out. There was no sign that anything was wrong, no visible indication of distress. Following the encounter, DD headed out to the farms that lay beyond his housing estate, entered a barn and hanged himself from a rafter. Anderson describes DD's death as 'drowning on dry land' (2020: 30). The phrase encapsulates the many deaths recounted in his memoir as, one after another, the men of his family silently drown, either on dry land or in the strong tidal currents of the River Foyle. There seems to be something intrinsic to Derry-Londonderry, something about the place where these men live, that causes one generation after another to succumb to the same silent, suffocating end.[1]

Anderson's maternal grandfather, Anthony, spent his working life on the River Foyle and he had an ability to chart it 'with a mapmaker's accuracy' (2020: 215). Whenever anyone went into the water, Anthony would go out to look for them. At the end of his life, Anthony found himself 'run aground' in a small room with relics of his nautical life washed up as 'flotsam' around him: among these objects, 'a broken barometer, fixed just shy of "Stormy"' (2020: 203). The barometer, an instrument used for measuring atmospheric pressure, becomes for Anderson a means of assessing the atmosphere in the city after the Troubles: there is, for him, something stuck, or broken, in Derry-Londonderry, like the barometer's needle that always points to 'Stormy'. Shortly after Anderson visits his grandfather to speak with him about his memories of the river, Anthony 'drowned in that airtight room' (2020: 219). Anderson evokes the phrase again to describe the death of his uncle, Budgie, noting that he too 'drown[ed] on dry land' (2020: 250). Budgie was in his thirties and homeless, and, with the refuge that he had been sleeping in closed to cut costs, he died of exposure in a disused public toilet. Anderson places DD's suicide alongside the deaths of Anthony and Budgie to produce a contextual narrative of the high suicide rates in Derry-Londonderry: cuts to services and high levels of poverty and mental illness constitute the prevailing atmosphere in which these men die. The city is bifurcated in complex ways, including religion and language, and it straddles the border between Northern Ireland and the Republic. The 'Bloody Sunday' incident of 1972 occurred in the Bogside area of the city, and Derry-Londonderry was severely affected by the Troubles.[2] Its inhabitants are cut loose from community ties in multiple, intersecting ways, and suicide becomes, for Anderson, a barometer of the poor social cohesion in the city.[3]

Inventory records a series of drownings in the River Foyle. Evoking the cliché that '[e]veryone knows where they were when Kennedy was shot',

Anderson notes that his paternal grandfather, Joseph, 'was drowning' (2020: 121). According to family legend, Joseph had staggered drunkenly off the docks, was knocked unconscious when a lifebuoy thrown out to rescue him struck him on the head and had disappeared into the river's depths. Joseph's drinking started when he returned from the Second World War, his death a final submergence by a war that had seen him sentenced to a military prison in England. After the Troubles, too, Anderson remarks that the Foyle was 'always there, beckoning the lost to escape to somewhere else' (2020: 317). In a culture that mandated silence even after the conflict, there was a 'deluge' (2020: 318) of suicides with almost one attempt taking place every night. Anderson repeatedly returns to the river to figure Derry-Londonderry as a place that catches young men in its deadly currents and drags them under the surface:

> There was simply no future for them, or rather the sense of no future prevailed. Their reasons were complex and nuanced and individual in each case, but there were certain universals. A sense of despair. An absence of any opportunity for a better life. The vertigo that might come at considering leaving the city, and the anger that came with having to. ... They were the left-behind in a city left behind.
>
> (2020: 317)

Anderson's memoir is an inventory of objects, including his grandfather's cracked barometer, through which he tells the story of growing up in Derry-Londonderry. The narrative that he uncovers comprises a different inventory: an archive of the dead. This inventory is held together by the ongoing effects of poverty and war that have claimed as many lives to suicide after the Troubles as were lost during the conflict itself.

Anderson ends his narrative with the disappearance of another cousin, Andrew. Andrew's wallet, keys and mobile phone are found on a bridge over the River Foyle, and a search party is called out to look for him along the riverbank. Anderson joins his father, who has already lost both of his parents to the river, and wonders what he is thinking as he returns 'once again, to retrieve the dead' (2020: 308). Anthony haunts Anderson's thoughts as he gazes out over the water because he 'would have known how to read the river, how to find the boy' (2020: 313). As the weather turns and a low front comes in, Anderson recalls the cracked barometer: 'The barometer in my grandfather's attic was stirring in the dark' (2020: 323). His father returns home, but Anderson continues to search for the body through the stormy night. He eventually receives a text to let him know that Andrew's body has been found close to the town and taken back to his mother. Sitting on the riverbank as darkness falls once more, Anderson picks up a small piece of driftwood from the shore and thinks of the human flotsam washed up along its banks: 'There was no ending to it. In a day or two, another young fella would be reported missing or seen going into the river. There is nothing to do but offer each other – those who are left, those still trapped within this miracle – the possibility of a life worth living, in defiance of "No future"' (2020: 355). What hope there is lies in social, political and economic change; investment in the city that would enable its young inhabitants to imagine a liveable future for themselves. Anderson's approach to suicide prevention converges with that of Mark E. Button, who moves beyond the sociological mapping of suicide to more active intervention, arguing that '[t]he harm of suicide ... involves the social and material disparities that are part of the condition of suicidality as well as the deeper harm of persistently ignoring these unequal conditions' (2016: 278). A social-justice response to suicide would – for Anderson, as for Button – entail 'a more politically oriented approach to the structural conditions of suicide' (2016: 278).

Anderson makes visible the slow violence that has affected, and continues to affect, the inhabitants of Derry-Londonderry, alongside the more explosive and spectacular violence of the Troubles. Such a contextual approach to suicide foregrounds the need to address social inequities, but it also gives visibility to the specifically male body. Anu Salmela indicates that this gendered phenomenon originated in the nineteenth century when 'female suicides [were portrayed] as individual, emotional acts ..., whereas male suicides were attributed to financial problems, unrealised ambitions and other factors linked to the state of the national economy and social wellbeing' (2018: 2). The health of a community – a nation or a city – was mapped on to the male suicidal body and vice versa. Katrina Jaworski identifies the legacy of these gendered norms in contemporary approaches to suicide, arguing: 'Emotional weakness and internal turmoil are seen as significant in interpreting women's suicides as a result of relationship breakdowns. In contrast, men's suicides are signs of courage, pride and resistance against external circumstances such as loss of employment or severe physical illness' (2014: 25). Jaworski acknowledges, however, that some recent studies have begun to interpret suicide outside of traditional gender configurations, connecting women's suicides to 'socioeconomic hardships' and recognizing that some men end their lives 'as a result of relationship breakdown' (2014: 28). Building on Jaworski's work, Ana Jordan and Amy Chandler observe that the current framing of suicide is problematic in its reliance on 'simplistic and binaristic models of gender, obscuring complexity and diverting attention from the existence and potentialities of multiple masculinities/femininities' (2019: 463). Further, they contend that the prevailing rhetoric of a crisis of masculinity 'renders invisible high levels of distress experienced by, and the costs of masculinity for, women' (2019: 471).

In *Thin Places*, ní Dochartaigh explicitly situates Derry-Londonderry as 'a hollowed-out place' (2021: 52). Like Anderson, ní Dochartaigh considers the atmosphere of the city to be set at stormy, but its pressure has recently intensified due to Brexit:

> We are, I fear, in the very eye of the storm. All around me shops lie empty, car bombs have started to go off again on our doorsteps, EU funding has been pulled out of youth groups, addiction units and much more, even before the UK has officially left the EU. ... Already the young folk in Derry stand even less chance of getting on in life than they did before.
>
> (2021: 34)

If the River Foyle fascinated Anderson for its depth, it attracts ní Dochartaigh as a boundary line that marks a religious, political and cultural divide. With Brexit, she contends, the river will 'shape-shift once more, to become a customs post: a threshold that must be crossed to pass from one place to the other' (2021: 56). In Anderson, the Foyle marked the threshold between life and death for the men who entered its waters; now, the hard border between Northern Ireland and the Republic threatens to materialize in physical form once again.

Thin Places is interested in what it means to come from such a place, asking: 'What effect does where you come from ... have on the map of your self?' (2021: 52). In relating her own suicide attempts to the place in which she grew up, ní Dochartaigh's narrative focuses on her bifurcated identity as the daughter of a Catholic mother and a Protestant father: *who* she is defines her relation to the city and exposes her to stigma, social exclusion, poor social support and poverty. The River Foyle marked out where the lines of the city were drawn, 'where your individual background allowed you to safely walk' (2021: 7). Catholics from one side of the river had no contact with Protestants on the other bank – they 'went to school separately, to church, sports events, funerals and pubs separately' (2021: 7). Ní Dochartaigh's childhood was spent ricocheting from one side of the river to the other, as her family was repeatedly burned and bullied out of the houses in which they lived. Her fractured identity is mirrored in the doubled name of Derry-Londonderry, a fault line along which the city threatens to divide once more as Brexit looms.[4]

Ní Dochartaigh writes her female body into the city's geography of despair: she, too, was submerged under the 'layer upon layer of despondency and helplessness' (2021: 50) that weighed upon the inhabitants of Derry-Londonderry. Like other young people, she was 'forced to leave' (2021: 108) the city because staying was not an option. Unable to see a future for herself, or to 'keep [her] head above water' (2021: 177), ní Dochartaigh tried to end her life by drowning in the River Lee, which flows through Cork, the city where she was then living. Her memoir records four separate suicide attempts before she knew that she had to leave that city, too, behind. *Thin Places* reminds us that it is not only young men who fall through the cracks that are exposed by violence and poverty. In relating people to place, we need to attend carefully to who becomes visible, and who does not, and to consider whose stories might potentially be excluded by focusing suicide through this lens.

The title of ní Dochartaigh's memoir refers to her grandfather's belief in 'thin places' (2021: 23), locations where 'you are allowed to cross any borders, where borders and boundaries hold no sway' (2021: 12). Thin places can be found anywhere and represent not just wild places but the most ordinary urban settings: 'supermarket carparks with even just one tree, the back of housing estates where life has been left to exist, ... dirty streams at the edges of things – full of waste but still brimming with something like renewal' (2021: 24). The most abandoned and broken places – like Derry-Londonderry itself – are also places of hope: ní Dochartaigh asserts that '[t]here are places that are both hollowed and hallowed all in one' (2021: 71). The River Foyle becomes the iconic thin place in her memoir. There, the boundary between living and dead is porous, 'thin as moth-wing' (2021: xii). The river cannot be contained by, and does not recognize, the artificial human borders imposed upon it. The freezing over of the Foyle in 1963 represents, in ní Dochartaigh's eyes, a nick in time when it momentarily revealed an alternative possibility for the divided city, as men and boys from both sides of the river played football matches on its surface, many of them venturing to the other side of the city for the first and only time in their lives. In that moment, ní Dochartaigh writes, 'All historical and imagined boundaries the river normally created were now displaced, dislocated, hidden from ... view' (2021: 57). By focusing suicide through thin places, ní Dochartaigh challenges the idea that suicide marks only the failure or collapse of the social. She conceives the relation of suicide to place, also, as potentially generative, offering a possible reimagining of the social, political and cultural life of the city.

Like Anderson, ní Dochartaigh closes her memoir with the disappearance of a young man into the waters of the Foyle. The search party concentrated their efforts on where he was thought to have entered the water: the place where the city becomes a boggy estuary. Ní Dochartaigh focuses her attention on the search party itself, as all the city's inhabitants come out to find his body: 'Folk from both sides of that river – Protestant and Catholic, political and apolitical – trudged through deep mud, along dark black tracks' (2021: 187). On the morning after the body has been found, washed up on the edge lands of the city, ní Dochartaigh observes that the votive candles, which had been lit during the search by the Catholic community on the Protestant side of the river where the boy was from, still burn in memory of him. Once again, the river allows an alternative future for the city to be glimpsed, rather than following the determined course of violence and division. In that moment, ní Dochartaigh experiences hope that the needle of the barometer is indeed stirring: 'I felt a change in the air … in that city of mine, despite the chaos and uncertainty that Brexit is blowing in on stormy winds' (2021: 191). The search party demonstrates a collective refusal to leave one of its own behind, to abandon the young man to the river. The vigil candle asserts that his life, like all the others who have entered these waters, carries meaning across the city. Judith Butler has observed of bodies assembling on the streets of a city in public acts of remembrance that 'the material history of … structures … works on them, becoming part of their very action' (2015: 85). The vigil candles were placed on the Peace Bridge, which was constructed over the Foyle in 2011 to improve access and relations between east and west sides of the city. The placement of the candles relates the young man's death to the ongoing story of Derry-Londonderry after the Troubles and suggests that his suicide might represent not only the end of a life but also new ways for those who remain to live together.

The needle of the barometer might be stirring, too, in my own hometown of Middlesbrough. If I now stand on the spot where I took the photograph of the Stray, the scene behind me is changing. The former steelworks are being dismantled and the site cleared. The land will be converted for the manufacture of wind turbines. There is hope that this will bring investment and employment to the area, combined with fear that a skilled workforce might be brought in from elsewhere and that the young will still struggle to envisage a liveable future. Even if the development benefits some, it will inevitably leave others behind, returning us to the question of who one is, as well as where one is from, in relating suicide to place. Hope for meaningful change remains fragile amid the economic uncertainty that will be left in the wake not only of Brexit but also the Coronavirus pandemic. There is, nevertheless, a tangible shift in the atmosphere, comparable to the change in the air that ní Dochartaigh discerned in her native Derry-Londonderry, which arises not only from external investment but also in the emergence of grassroots networks of solidarity and support.[5]

I regard the Stray as one of ní Dochartaigh's thin places. It is heavily industrialized, but the natural world has found a way to flourish there. With groynes preventing the sands from disappearing into the water, the beach is precariously positioned between land and sea. It is a place where the boundary between the living and the dead feels slight, almost indiscernible – like the sea frets that can descend there in any season. I have so far considered how place might be considered a factor in suicide, but the place where a suicide occurs can also map onto the bereaved in affective and emotional terms. I therefore turn in the following section to consider the relation between place and grief, drawing on ideas of place as layered, embodied and shifting to explore a variety of informal practices of suicide memorialization.

A wooden bench

Louise Doughty's *Platform Seven* opens with the striking description of a man's suicide at Peterborough Railway Station. It is four in the morning and the station is empty, except for the staff on night duty and a lone fox that trots along the tracks before leaping up onto Platform Two and disappearing into the dark. The talismanic appearance of the fox marks out the ordinary space of Peterborough station as one of the thin places: in Doughty's terms, the station is 'a portal' and '[t]he dividing line between life and the afterlife is porous here' (2019: 42). The novel's narrator speaks to us from the afterlife: she has already died on Platform Seven and is caught within the station grounds, watching those who work there and those who pass through without being visible to them. Platform Seven is the most recent extension to the station, and it is 'the furthest from the entrance, from the Duty Team Leader's office and the Customer Information Point' (2019: 7). The narrator comes across the man 'sitting on [a] metal bench' (2019: 7). As a freight train approaches, he moves to the edge of the platform and falls forward onto the tracks, oblivious to the security guard's frantic attempts to prevent him on the opposite platform.

Doughty's narrative focus is on the procedures that follow the man's death, which act as a powerful reminder of Lisa Stevenson's observation, quoted in Chapter 1, that the clock 'has no time for suicide' (2014: 147). As soon as the incident is reported to the Fatality Hotline and the trains are stopped, the 'ninety-minute rule' applies (2019: 19), which refers to the permitted interval for the removal of body parts and the reopening of the line. The first train running from Peterborough Station that morning is the 06.10 to Birmingham New Street, and the station is to be open at the usual time of 06.00. Doughty mitigates the bureaucratic protocol by highlighting how the various people whose jobs bring them into contact with the man's suicide are affected by it. The duty officer for the British Transport Police assists the Specialist Cleaning Unit to carry the body bag from the platform to the Dignity van at the front of the station and is 'proud of the fact that he … has not cried' (2019: 21). Melissa, the station manager, talks to all her staff as soon as she arrives on duty at 08.00 and then goes to Platform Seven to pay her respects to the dead. Suicide is brought into the everyday through the familiar rhythms and routines of the station and in Doughty's close attention to the decidedly mundane spaces that comprise the immediate environs of Platform Seven: Pumpkin Café, the West Cornwall Pasty Company shop, the Duty Team Leader's office.

As she braces herself to go to Platform Seven, Melissa recalls the previous death on the line – which was that of the narrator – and her encounter with the young woman's parents three days later, when they 'clutch[ed] a small bouquet of pink and white roses … that they wanted to lay at the end of the platform' (2019: 29). Melissa explains to the parents and their Family Liaison Officer that, even though their tribute is modest, they cannot place the flowers on the platform 'because of the risk of copycat incidents' (2019: 29). Even though she has followed the protocols, the incident haunts Melissa, and she wonders whether she could have reached a compromise, 'leaving [the flowers] on the Information Desk, perhaps – somewhere where it would be … normal to have flowers' (2019: 30). She accordingly accompanies the son and daughter of the man who has ended his life to Platform Seven and stands with them 'as they stare down into the four-foot in their moment of silent homage' (2019: 379). Doughty captures the tension surrounding those suicidal deaths which occur in public places between the desire of the bereaved to pay their respects at the place where the death occurred and injunctions against memorialization, lest it should lead to further suicides at that location.[6]

Avril Maddrell has noted that most deaths in the contemporary global north take place in 'an institution, such as a hospital, hospice or care home', meaning that typically 'contact with the institution naturally comes to an end at the time of death' (2016: 174). A minority of deaths, including some suicides, occur in 'a location not usually associated with death, e.g., ... road, beach or bridge' (2016: 174). Augustine J. Kposowa and James P. McElvain point out that, in some instances of suicide, the place of death might be recorded as an institution, even though the suicide attempt took place at a different location:

[N]ot all attempts of suicide cause immediate death. Depending on the method employed, the victim may be rendered unconscious and discovered by a friend or family member before succumbing to death. ... Under such circumstances, police and paramedics are routinely summoned to the location to provide aid and treatment to the victim by transporting him or her to a hospital. Despite efforts to sustain the victim's life, not all attempts succeed, and the victim dies at the hospital. In other situations, even though the discovered victim may display no vital signs, as long as there are no obvious indications of death ... it is common for emergency responders to attempt to revive the victim and transport him or her to a hospital. ... As a result, the official recorded place of death becomes the hospital where the victim was delivered, and not where the suicide event began.

(2020: 437)

For Kposowa and McElvain, the place of suicide comprises 'where the suicide event took place' (2020: 437), even though this may not be the location recorded on the death certificate.[7] For my purposes, this is the place onto which suicide grief is commonly mapped because of its more intimate association with the actions and intentions of the deceased.

When the place of suicide is a public space, the bereaved may have to encounter it regularly. The location can become associated with a personalized ritual of remembrance, which enables it to be integrated into the everyday movements of the bereaved. The narrator of *Platform Seven* first notices the dead man's son in the Pumpkin Café because he is unable to enter the station as if there is 'some invisible force field preventing him' (2019: 51). When he does eventually move through the station barriers, he heads directly to the metal bench on Platform Seven. He steps to the edge of the platform as a freight train approaches, seeking an understanding of what his father's death might have been like. He then returns to his daily commute, catching the Stowmarket train from Platform Six at 07.30, and the narrator observes that '[t]he station seems to hold no terrors for him now' (2019: 107). Shortly after this, he stands on Platform Seven with his sister and Melissa in a more formalized ritual of remembrance. Platform Seven is a place he cannot avoid, and it requires careful negotiation and ritualization.

Travelling north from Peterborough to York, we encounter another bench on a station platform, this time seen through the eyes of Avril Maddrell:

> Waiting for a train, … I sat on an unusual bench. … It was crafted from oak by Robert 'Mouseman' Thompson, with his signature mouse carved underneath the armrest, and was dedicated in memory of a woman who died at 38 years of age. In addition to the craftsmanship of the woodwork and the poignancy of a (by western standards) fore-shortened life, I was struck by the inscription: 'Still Travelling'. From the perspective of the bereaved she was still 'alive', her absence due to being on a journey 'elsewhere'. No doubt the form, location and text of the memorial tell us something of the deceased's identity, but it also speaks of her vitality in the present.
>
> (2013: 502)

This bench, which is made of wood rather than of metal, commemorates an employee of the railway company who worked at the headquarters in York and died suddenly of a brain tumour. On Platform One of Darlington Railway Station, another 'Mouseman' bench memorializes the dead of the Yorkshire Regiment, its location chosen because the regiment regularly travels through the station to train at nearby Catterick Garrison.[8] These wooden benches comprise what Maddrell has termed 'vernacular memorials' (2012: 47), which typically take the form of benches, trees and plaques and which 'have become a tradition in their own right, especially in relation to untimely or tragic death' (2012: 47). Evoking nature and the handcrafted and incorporating 'popular culture and the idiom of everyday life' (2012: 47), these memorials are regularly encountered, and their locations often reflect a place that was special to the deceased. Doughty's metal bench might be parsed in contrast with these wooden memorial benches – its standardized, industrial manufacture means that flowers or other tributes laid nearby would appear out of place. They would call attention not to the dead but to the location as a site of death.

The Channel 4 documentary, *Caroline Flack: Her Life and Death* (2021), addresses the high-profile suicide of the media star in February 2020, from the perspective of her family and friends. The film closes with Flack's family walking to the memorial bench by which they have commemorated her, which is located on a wooded path overlooking a scenic vista. Her mother talks to the camera as they approach the bench, observing that it affords a place where it is possible simply to sit and remember. The comfort that the bench affords is connected to place and to the object's tangible presence. Touching the arm of the bench, Flack's mother remarks that it seems somehow to embody her dead daughter, and her gesture echoes the act of reaching out to the arm of another person in the course of a conversation. The bench carries a metaphoric relation to the dead, and it represents Flack's ongoing vitality for her family, its carved inscription foregrounding her life rather than the manner of her death. Such wooden benches afford what Leonie Kellaher and Ken Worpole have termed a 'lo[w]-key form of contemporary memorialisation' (2010: 161):

> Rest, tranquillity and a certain measured continuity appear to be intended. ... The ... wooden benches are crafted from the material provided by their alternative, the growing tree: one carries a message of stability and stasis, as well as human investment in its shaping and emplacement; the other signifies a trust that nature will grow and regenerate so that the memory can be sustained and develop.
>
> (2010: 162)

The siting of the memorial bench dedicated to Caroline Flack on a public footpath means that others will regularly pass by and remember, the bench unobtrusively locating the family's loss in relation to an expanded community of walkers, runners and dog walkers.

Maddrell notes of the ubiquity of vernacular memorials in our common spaces that 'the[y] inflect our experience and understanding of these landscapes' (2013: 510). In the context of suicide, these understated memorials enable the death to be made visible in a way that does not invite further stigma. Vernacular memorials might be conceptualized in relation to Kathleen Stewart's ordinary affect, bringing into view how encounters with them can potentially be productive of personal and social change. For Stewart, ordinary affects register through 'rhythms of flow and arrest' (2007: 19). The memorial provokes a response and, through this reaction, '[i]t will shift people's life trajectories in some small way, change them by literally changing their course for a minute or a day' (2007: 12). A pause, a rest, a detour: these minor actions comprise for Stewart a momentary surrender of the self and of agency, as the affective charge of something encountered passes through the body, making the passer-by an involuntary participant in its world. Returning to Sara Ahmed's vocabulary of orientation discussed in Chapter 1, these memorials divert us from the straight line, they pull us momentarily off course, and in so doing they can act as a means of reorientation. Vernacular memorials solicit, in Stewart's words, 'some kind of intimate public of onlookers [to] recognize something in a space of shared impact' (2007: 39). There is accordingly a politics in how we structure our movements in relation to them, patterning our behaviour according to our engagement with, avoidance of or indifference to their interpellation of us.

A wooden memorial bench acts as a repository of feeling, which is encoded not only in its physical form and placement but also in those objects that are left there, freighted with emotional significance. These flowers, photographs and messages have a more improvised feel than those left at a graveside, lacking the formality of the surrounding cemetery. In this sense, vernacular memorials conform to Ann Cvetkovich's 'archive of feelings' (2003: 7), a term that she has used to register 'moments of everyday emotional distress' alongside 'moments of extreme trauma' (2003: 3). Her project is congruent with my approach to suicide in its attempt to capture 'a sense of trauma as connected to the textures of everyday experience' (2003: 3–4). Cvetkovich observes of the performances and rituals that materialize in and around vernacular memorials: '[They] displac[e] the dyadic and hierarchical relationship between doctor and patient that governs clinical approaches to trauma, opening that relationship out into the public sphere and expanding the repertoire for the expression of emotion. When culture takes over from the clinic, … it continues to perform therapeutic functions, but these functions are embedded within collective and public practices' (2003: 286). Memorial benches bring into focus the agency and creativity of the bereaved, who engage in their own acts of sense- and meaning-making and map out personal emotional topographies. Vernacular memorials braid the movements of the bereaved into the familiar routes and circuits of commuters and pedestrians: their feelings are thereby implicated in the quotidian lives of others, and, as local landmarks, these memorials constellate the kinds of 'intimate public' to which Stewart refers (2007: 39).

My sister's death certificate records the place of her death as 'The Beach, Redcar'. The Stray is not somewhere I regularly encounter; getting there takes me out of my way, and every visit since my sister's death has therefore been an intentional act of remembrance. There are vernacular memorials at the beach: the wooden benches lining the seafront have dedicatory plaques commemorating loved ones, and I have come across bouquets of flowers tied to railings, not knowing whether they memorialized a road accident or a drowning – either way, their presence marks the location as the site of another untimely death. I have struggled to know how to commemorate my sister at the place where she died: every gesture feels at once too much and not enough. There is no obvious place to leave flowers or other tributes, and the act of doing so feels incongruous amid the runners and the dog walkers. My sister's death left no visible trace, and I have struggled to connect it meaningfully to the site where it happened, to bridge the gap between the extraordinary and the everyday.

Maddrell has noted that places associated with mourning can change over time, moving away from the cemetery or the site of death to attach to other spaces. These locations might be actively designated as a memorial site, or they can take on an unexpected emotional significance, becoming 'affectively charged' in relation to a death (2015: 170). In my desire to connect my sister's death to a place, I turned to Crosby Sands, a two-mile stretch of beach on which one hundred cast-iron naked men stand gazing out to sea, in the sculptural installation that comprises Antony Gormley's *Another Place*. The title of Gormley's work gestures to the horizon at which these men stare out, directing our attention to the numinous. Standing among the sculptures for the first time, the title took on a different valence, as I felt that this place could readily be transposed onto the Stray. On my left, as I stood facing out to sea, was the port of Liverpool; ahead of me was an offshore wind farm; behind me was a seaside town which had fallen into the familiar state of disrepair.[9] The iron men disappearing into the sea all around me, first to their knees, then to their waists, then to their heads, and then completely, gave material form to my sister's body as she had walked into the sea, helping me to connect her death to the humdrum reality of a windswept beach in northern England.

Gormley's installation gave me a place where I could go to remember my sister – a beach I could map onto, but that was not, the place of her death. I was not alone in responding to the sculptures in this way: several of the iron men had ritual objects placed on, around or beside them – football shirts and scarves, wristbands, flowers, pebbles – so that they already constituted a vernacular memorial for visitors to the beach, acting as the locus for a variety of commemorative practices. I did not add to the small gatherings of votive objects assembled at the installation, although I was consoled by their presence. The ritual act of walking barefoot along the stretch of beach, watching as the ebb tide retreated and the sculptures gradually reappeared, the sea giving them back to me as it receded down the sands, constituted its own practice of meaningful commemoration. The tide clock on my kitchen wall

(Figure 4), set to the rising and falling of the tides at Crosby Beach, enables me to visualize at a glance whether the sculptures are being submerged or uncovered by the sea. The clock brings the ritual act of memorialization into my domestic space, integrating it into my everyday habit and routine.

Vernacular memorials materialize grief in a place; they also materialize grief as a posture. The memorial bench thus produces an embodied relationship to the dead that entails sitting down to remember. Gormley's silently contemplative iron men stand straight and upright and apparently require no support to maintain this position, despite being covered by the sea at each high tide. In fact, the vertical posture of the iron men is reliant on two-metre steel piles, which are driven into the sand below each of the sculptures. Gormley's installation lines the men into rows so that, walking on the beach, I became conscious of whether I was in line, or in alignment, with them. The positioning as well as the posture of the iron men might be read, in Ahmed's terms, as a 'straightening device', which 'keep[s] things in line … by "holding" things in place' (2006b: 66). We stay upright, the sculptures suggest, we hold the line, and we fix our gaze on what lies ahead: their lesson is one of stoic endurance.

Even with their invisible supports, some of the iron men have inclined at different angles, and one or two of them more nearly approach the horizontal than the vertical axis. Adriana Cavarero has called attention to the inclined subject as the figure for a 'relational ontology' (2016: 10), contrasting it to the upright and autonomous, free-standing figure which dominates the Western imagination. For Ahmed, a queer phenomenology necessarily entails taking up such an angle such that 'the world itself might appear on a slant, which disorientates the picture and even unseats the body' (2006b: 67). Viewed in this light, the inclined figures at Crosby, knocked off balance by the waves and the shifting sands, are suggestive of a version of grief that can be productively disorientating and destabilizing. For Judith Butler, discussed in Chapter 2, grief uncovers the extent to which we are held together by our relationships so that losing a loved one produces a fundamental shift in our sense of gravity and a corresponding loss of equilibrium. Whenever I visit Crosby, I deliberately seek out these leaning figures with their curious, slantwise perspectives on the world.[10] Their torqued, tilted and angled postures inscribe grief's loss of direction, its inherent instability, which might, in Ahmed's terms, 'be lived purely as loss' or which might, alternatively, 'redirect us and open up new worlds' (2006b: 19).

Maddrell has charted in medical and health geography a 'shif[t] from studying dots on maps to embodied subjects' (2015: 169). This chapter has likewise moved from an initial focus on the demographic mapping of suicide onto place to asking how grief is enacted by the bereaved in specific sites and places. Gormley's sculptural installation at Crosby Sands has helped me to map my own grief onto place, as well as to experience an embodied and situated relation to my sister's death. Jo Carruthers and Nour Dakkak have encouraged visitors to Crosby not to follow the gaze of the iron men out to the horizon, but rather to focus their attention on 'the sand in which they stand' (2020: 1). Looking down, they argue, brings into focus 'sandscapes [as] messy places' (2020: 7). The sandscape of Crosby Beach comprises a dangerous area of tidal mud and quicksand. Steven Connor has opined that, if sand is 'the most untrustworthy [of matters], the most shifting and shifty', then quicksand is even more treacherous, 'doubl[ing] the dubiousness of what is already an uncertain substance' (2010: no pagination). Maddrell has described the project of mapping grief in similar terms, viewing it as 'a window on to the messy, shifting, multi-layered geographies of living with loss' (2015: 184). The topographies of grief are fluid and uncertain, and they involve stasis and stuckness as well as mobility and movement. They are comprised of the fleeting, the ephemeral and the temporary, and they are hard to capture without fixing them into place. They are, for these very reasons, significant in relation to suicide because they afford a glimpse of the material, sensory and affective practices of the bereaved. They allow the bereaved to make sense out of loss and to situate their grief in relation to wider social and community landscapes.

Communities of care

The twenty-first century has witnessed a shift not only in practices of grieving, which are moving away from the cemetery to more personal and vernacular sites of mourning, but also in clinical conceptualizations of the process of grieving. Twentieth-century models of mourning in the West were premised on the bereaved working through a series of distinct and identifiable stages of grief towards resolution, which was manifested in a separation from, or a letting go of, the deceased. Grief had a definable path or trajectory and was understood to be a linear progression through recognizable temporalities of mourning. Those who did not conform to this normative model of grief could find that their experiences of loss were pathologized, and an ongoing attachment to the dead might be classified as a depressive symptom or labelled as an abnormal reaction. For Anna

Harpin, the Diagnostic and Statistical Manual has extended this time-limited approach to grief into the present, while also compressing the permitted timescale for the working-through of emotion: 'Grief … has an ever-shrinking proscribed shelf-life. Our moods, now, are, like our bodies, on the clock' (2018: 176). This subordination of the temporalities of grief to clock time is symptomatic of the neoliberalization of contemporary health care, which requires the bereaved to take individual responsibility for their own resilience and well-being in the face of loss. Harpin's point is an important one, and I do not want to confuse the agency of the bereaved in the following discussion with a neoliberal delegation of responsibility for care. Rather, I turn to the therapeutic framework of grieving based on the idea of continuing bonds, which has also entered the mainstream, and which accommodates a more fluid and ongoing relationality to the dead, in order to trace out some of the grassroots communities of care that can materialize in the wake of suicide.

Dennis Klass et al. published the seminal *Continuing Bonds: New Understandings of Grief* in 1996, arguing for an urgent reassessment of the dominant understanding of grief as the cutting of bonds with the deceased. Based in clinical practice, the volume contended that, at the end of treatment, 'what we were observing was not a stage of disengagement, which we were educated to expect, but rather, we were observing people altering and then continuing their relationship to the lost or dead person' (1996: xviii). The existing theoretical model did not map onto what was happening in the consulting room, as the bereaved maintained relational bonds to the dead. Klass et al. proposed that such an ongoing, evolving and active engagement with the deceased was itself normative and could continue throughout a person's life. With this change of focus came the need for a new vocabulary to describe how we 'talk about and to the deceased' (1996: 19) and how that language might alter over time.[11] Bereavement was now premised on a continuing social relationship between mourner and deceased, leading Jo Bell et al. to observe that 'grief represents a shifting social encounter and connection' (2015: 376).

Yiyun Li's *Where Reasons End* affords a helpful starting point for thinking further about the continuing bond between mourner and deceased in the context of suicide. As discussed in Chapter 2, Li's narrator addresses her dead son directly and maintains with him the kind of conversation that she would have had in life. Her ongoing dialogue with the dead is evocative of online memorial practices, which have become an important mode of memorialization in relation to suicidal deaths because they provide space to express an often-stigmatized grief. Read in this light, Li's novel could be seen to explore not only the language of cliché but also the idiom of mourning that is emerging out of online suicide memorial sites. So ubiquitous have such online memorial pages become that Louis Bailey et al. have asked, '[D]o we now have an additional space within the contemporary spiritual psyche – the ethereal space of the Internet – where the bereaved linger and continue to interact with the deceased?' (2015: 85). Li creates an equivalent space within the contemporary novel, which permits the narrator to linger with her dead son, and for their loving and quarrelsome conversation to unfold.

Those bereaved by suicide can create a memorial on dedicated online platforms, which are created specifically to commemorate those who die from a particular illness or type of death – alongside suicide, Karolina Kryskinska and Karl Andriessen have identified sites that are dedicated to breast cancer, AIDS and sudden infant death syndrome (2015: 22), and miscarriage and stillbirth could be added to their inventory. These platforms comprise online versions of the cemetery and their features are designed to resemble traditional mourning rites, combining the grave as a space of mourning which can be visited and where tributes can be placed, and the book of condolence where photographs, biographies, readings from funerals, blogs and messages might be posted. Kryskinska and Andriessen have observed that messages dedicated to those who died from suicide 'more frequently include information about the cause of death, a wish that the deceased might (finally) rest in peace, and the attempts to understand and come to terms with the loss' (2015: 23). In addition to maintaining a continuing bond with the dead, the online memorial platform makes the deceased visible within a community of others who have died in the same way, and it can accrue a political dimension in calling attention to the scale of deaths by suicide or another type of death. The online memorial site is, in this sense, poised between private and public commemoration. It offers formalized tropes for remembrance, and it provides, in Maddrell's terms, a valuable 'space for socially marginalised bereavements' (2012: 49).

Social-media sites, and Facebook in particular, have provided an alternative setting for online grieving practices, which is at once more personal and less formalized than dedicated online platforms, as well as already being integrated into the everyday life of the deceased and the bereaved. Bailey et al. found in their study of online memorial practices that Facebook 'was by far the most commonly used resource' among those bereaved by suicide (2015: 75). Some mourners chose to create a new Facebook page to commemorate the deceased, while others kept and sustained existing

Facebook accounts belonging to the person who had died. In the latter instance, Bell et al. observe that the timeline relating to the deceased's life is visible, as well as her 'likes and dislikes, status, favourite quotations, songs, video clips and conversations' (382). Suicide violently severs the timeline of the deceased. Facebook enables it to continue, albeit differently, as the bereaved post memories and conversations and upload photographs and video clips. Bailey et al. report that continuing bonds are central to maintaining existing Facebook sites: '[T]he most common motivating factor was the need to … *keep the deceased alive*' (2015: 78). Li has asked how a memorial might capture the animation of those who are no longer there, and uploaded recordings and clips on Facebook arguably reproduce this aspect of the dead more successfully than traditional memorial objects.

Facebook also facilitates communities of care among the living. Pages created to commemorate those who have died by suicide often incorporate information about relevant support groups and promote fundraising activities or campaigns for related organizations. Bell et al. note that social-networking platforms alleviate the potential isolation of suicide bereavement by connecting mourners to 'others in a similar position (who they might not otherwise meet)' (2015: 378). Existing Facebook profiles act as a vehicle for communicating the news of the death, as they provide an effective means of contacting wider networks outside the family. Bailey et al. observe that '[t]he instantaneous nature of Facebook mean[s] that news about the death spread[s] relatively quickly and save[s] the bereaved from having to make a series of difficult phone calls to people who they [a]re not otherwise close to or in touch with' (75). Facebook activity is most intensive in the months following the death as those affected engage in a collective sharing of photographs, comments and links. Bell et al. note that this communication is 'a shared social activity mediated often by those closest to the deceased but also in contributions from those belonging to wider social networks' (2015: 382). By posting photographs, anecdotes and video clips, this wider community add new memories of the deceased to what is already known and familiar.[12] In addition to creating a living memorial, the community of mourners is held together by quotidian rhythms and routines, leading Bell et al. to suggest that care is shaped by 'the ways in which mourners come and go online' (2015: 383). Returning to Kathleen Stewart's ordinary affect, Facebook constellates a virtual 'intimate public' (2007: 39) around the dead, which is felt and experienced through online 'rhythms of movement and arrest' (2007: 19).

Online memorialization typically follows immediately on from the death. In some experiences of grief, a more involved relationship with the deceased might emerge after an interval of time has elapsed. Klass et al. explain that, when a loss occurs in early adulthood, it will often be revisited later in life, as 'th[e] understanding of who died will evolve and change' over time (1996: 352). In *Evelyn*, Orlando von Einsiedel records his own and his siblings' grieving process thirteen years after their brother took his own life. The three remaining siblings – Orlando, the eldest; Gwennie, his sister; and younger brother, Robin – remember their brother as they walk together in places that they had shared with Evelyn. On different walks, the siblings are joined by other family members and by Evelyn's closest friends. The film charts the continuing bonds the siblings have with Evelyn, and it documents their collective movement towards a new perspective on their brother's death, as well as its integration into their familial and social relationships. The documentary does not, however, work towards the resolution of grief: Robin reflects on the South Downs that '[i]t doesn't mean we're done with it. We should make this an ongoing discussion'. Rather, von Einsiedel probes the ways in which the family acts as a site in which suicide is materialized in the everyday, and through which its meanings are both constructed and contested. Relating suicide, von Einsiedel reminds us, is also about who we are related to.

Sara Ahmed has memorably described the kitchen table as an object around which the family orients itself. It is, she observes, an object 'around which bodies gather, cohering as a group through the "mediation" of its surface' (2006b: 80). Food and conversation are shared around the table, which becomes, in its familiarity, a part of the family: 'the table becomes a relative' (2006b: 81). Gathering around the table is not a neutral activity, however; it both aligns and keeps in line:

> Around [the kitchen table] we gather every morning and evening.
> Each of us has our own place. Mine is the end of the table opposite
> my father. My sisters are both to my left, my mother to my right. Each
> time we gather in this way, as if the arrangement is securing more than
> our place. For me, inhabiting the family is about taking up a place
> already given. I slide into my seat and take up this place. I feel out of
> place in this place, but these feelings are pushed to one side. We can
> consider how families are often about taking sides (one side of the
> table or another) and how this requirement 'to side' requires putting
> other things aside.
>
> (2006b: 88–9)

The walks around which *Evelyn* is structured remove the family from the fixed places of the kitchen table, yet its configurations continually encroach on their interactions. The picnic lunch on the siblings' first walk with their mother, Beta, in the Cairngorms National Park, fades into a family photograph with Evelyn taken on the same spot in 1995. The family have taken up their places in relation to their dead brother and son, as if to secure him in place once more. Evelyn's death has left what Orlando names a 'void' in the family, around which their identities have become as static as the pose in the photograph.

The siblings' walk in the Lake District with their father and stepmother, Andreas and Jo, begins with Jo observing 'an enormous amount of tension in the air'; the stormy atmosphere centres on Gwennie and her father. An argument breaks out between them when Andreas positions his children on one side of the family (table) or the other, identifying Gwennie with the maternal line and Evelyn with his own, paternal German inheritance. Jo's prediction that 'something will explode' is realized that evening when the family gather around a restaurant table, and Gwennie objects to Andreas's criticism of the service. The siblings are on one side of the table, and Andreas and Jo face them on the other. Robin steps out of alignment by encouraging Gwennie to put her feelings aside, which means that she can continue to take her place at the family table. The integration into the film of drone camera footage, with its overhead perspective of the family walks, further highlights whether the family is in line with each other or if they have fallen out of step, fracturing into separate conversations. Von Einsiedel makes painfully – and at times humorously – tangible the normative, as well as the normalizing, influence of family in the wake of suicide, and relationships strain to breaking point as the siblings struggle to voice what Evelyn's death has meant to them.

The family is surrounded and supported by a wider circle of intimates, who play a significant role in helping the siblings to reorient themselves in relation to Evelyn's death. The film crew for *Evelyn* comprised the same small unit which had worked with von Einsiedel on his two previous documentary films, *Virunga* (2014) and *The White Helmets* (2016): both films were shot in war zones under difficult circumstances, which had brought the team close together. In a post-screening discussion of *Evelyn* at the DocHouse in London, Gwennie observed how important it was to have producer Joanna Natasegara there, as 'someone from the outside' who could bring an external perspective to the familial tensions playing out on the walks. Evelyn's friend Leon performs an equivalent role on screen, when he walks with the siblings in the Trossachs. Leon takes up with Orlando the emotional distress that

he, as director, has asked others to speak of and that he is now expecting his
siblings to discuss without ever articulating his own feelings:

> You're taking a liberty. You're going to have to talk. You're trying
> to hide behind asking questions and stuff. It's a touch of that stiff
> upper lip, man. … That's an outdated view of masculinity, and seeing
> someone like you, someone as successful as you are, being open and
> vulnerable, might make all the difference to someone watching this, to
> someone who is not able to talk about it for fear of being seen as weak.

Orlando responds that he is not afraid of appearing weak 'in front of anyone
except my sister'. His position in the family, reinforced after Evelyn's death,
is that of the strong older brother who holds everything together and puts
his own feelings aside. It is only after Leon's intervention that Orlando can
begin to reposition himself and manifest his own emotional vulnerability to
his younger siblings.

In *The Care Manifesto*, the Care Collective proposed an ethics of
'promiscuous care' (2020: 2). Expanding kinship beyond the family to friends,
neighbours, communities and more distant relationships, promiscuous care
'would enable us to *multiply* the numbers of people we can care for, about and
with, thus permitting us to *experiment* with the ways that we care' (2020: 2).
Care in *Evelyn* expands beyond the intimate circle of Evelyn's friends, as the
siblings encounter and converse with strangers on their walks, whose lives have
also been affected by suicide. In the Lake District, an ice-cream vendor lost his
mother to suicide four years ago, and he tells Orlando and Gwennie that he
and his sister celebrate her life every year on the anniversary of its ending. On
the South Downs, the siblings speak to an ex-soldier who has lost three of his
former comrades from the armed forces to suicide. In Scotland, a landlady is
running her brother's pub because he ended his life a month before. As well
as testifying to the pervasiveness of suicide in the everyday, these impromptu
exchanges negotiate a space of care that enables strangers to be touched by
Evelyn's death, as well as to share their own experiences of loss. The film maps
Evelyn's death not only onto the places that he loved but also in relation to
others' experiences of suicide bereavement that the siblings encounter there.

The circle of care in *Evelyn* also expands beyond the frame of the
screen to include the audience. The Care Collective observe that 'public
spaces are crucial for building caring communities because they … can
foster conviviality, interconnections and the emergence of communal life'
(2020: 49). Harnessing the public space of the cinema, the von Einsiedels
aimed to have a family member present at every regional screening of

Evelyn to participate in a discussion of the issues raised. At the DocHouse screening, Gwennie remarked that 'the Q&As ... have been so incredible. A lot of people want to share'. Where possible, screenings were organized as matinees so that, after the discussion, the family member could also participate in an organized walk, run in conjunction with the Ramblers' Association, for anyone who wanted to connect and talk further. The walks in the film thereby extended into local communities, and the family circle expanded to include those audience members who chose to take part. The post-screening walks fostered interconnection and sociality around suicide, facilitated by local support organizations.

Evelyn opens and closes with footage shot on the night of the last walk, in which Orlando opens and reads his brother's suicide note, which he has carried with him throughout the filming. Evelyn's letter to his family is, in Ahmed's terms, a sticky object. Found in Evelyn's pocket after he died, it acts as a material witness to the death, and it is accompanied by a letter from the coroner, marking its subsequent contact with the law. Orlando's opening of the letter thirteen years after Evelyn's death returns us to the question with which I began, namely, what does it mean to live beside suicide? Von Einsiedel adds an additional dimension to this question, asking, more specifically, what it means to live beside suicide *as a sibling*. *Evelyn* explores an overlooked aspect of suicide: the gap in siblings that it often leaves behind. Living beside suicide can mean sliding into an accustomed seat at the family table but feeling that it is not your place any longer. The very act of taking up a place at the table might mean putting aside feelings of grief and loss. *Evelyn* makes visible how difficult it is to reconfigure family relationships in the wake of suicide. I had no other siblings, and the death of my sister entailed not knowing whether I now still constituted a sister – even now, I often hesitate when I am asked if I have any siblings, weighing my desire to answer truthfully against the social appropriateness of the conversation that might ensue. My thirtieth birthday meant that I had not only outlived my sister but had also lived longer than her. Could I still count myself as the younger sister when I would always now be older than her, the gap between us widening with every passing year? Should I now slide into place as the older sister around the family table, or was that to take up a place that would always belong to my sister? In Chapter 2, I considered suicide bereavement as the relearning of simple nouns such as window, door and house. *Evelyn* adds more nouns to this list of words that acquire new meaning in the wake of suicide: table, brother, sister.

For Ahmed, the kitchen table forms part of the family. The last community of care that we might consider is therefore that which is provided by those objects which bear an intimate relation to us. This book has accumulated an archive of such objects: a watch, an alarm clock, a tide clock, a photograph, a cracked barometer, a wooden bench, a kitchen table, a letter. Ahmed is interested in how we are oriented towards such objects and in how they in turn help us to find our way. We are bound to everyday objects in forms of relation that take shape in our repeated and habitual encounters with them:

> Orientations are tactile and they involve more than one skin surface: we, in approaching this or that table, are also approached by the table, which touches us when we touch it. … This body with this table is a different body than it would be without it. And, the table is a different table when it is with me than it would be without me. Neither the object nor the body have integrity in the sense of being 'the same thing' with or without others. Bodies as well as objects take shape through being orientated toward each other, as an orientation that may be experienced as the co-habitation or sharing of space.
>
> (2006b: 54)

This book has attended to the ways in which grief is registered and experienced through the coming together of this body and this object. Suicide, I have suggested, takes shape in our ordinary interactions with benches and tables, with watches and barometers and letters: in the ways in which these objects touch us even as we touch them. The relating of suicide is accordingly a matter not only of who we are related to but also of what objects we claim or count as being among our kin.

Notes

1 Derry-Londonderry is a dramatically cut place; returning to Elizabeth Grosz's 'nicks' in time, we might usefully ask whether her concept could be expanded to include nicks or cuts in place – a possibility that ní Dochartaigh seems to gesture towards in her representation of the frozen-over River Foyle.

2 The Troubles, a thirty-year conflict, are commonly seen to have begun at a civil rights march in Derry-Londonderry in 1968, and to have formally ended with the signing of the Good Friday Agreement in 1998.

3 Although Anderson's paternal grandmother, Needles, also drowned in the River Foyle, her death is attributed by Anderson to individual rather than collective circumstance: diagnosed with cancer, Anderson indicates that she opted to die by drowning. Needles' drowning was recorded by the coroner as 'Death by Misadventure' – perhaps, Anderson notes, 'out of kindness … given the lingering Catholic idea of eternal limbo for the lost souls of those who have

taken their own lives' (2020: 150). Anderson's observation is a reminder that religious belief can also be entangled in suicide's materialization.

4   Ní Dochartaigh's attention to the border chimes with China Mills' understanding of suicide 'as linked to ongoing repetitive border struggles, including systems of administration and classification that are violent in both banal and spectacular ways', and that link to broader colonial and racial histories (2020: 83).

5   Examples of grassroots support initiatives on Teesside include the 'Teesside United' campaign, launched in 2021 by the Boro Walkers Association. The 'No Substitute' campaign was also launched in 2021 by Redcar and Cleveland Borough Council, in conjunction with the North Riding County Football Association, and uses football to raise awareness of mental-health problems in young men.

6   For example, the Public Health Agency for Northern Ireland has produced guidelines for families wishing to memorialize a loved one following a death by suicide. The advice concerning a public memorial such as a bench, plaque or mural reads as follows: 'If you wish to have a permanent memorial, we would advise that this is placed at a private location such as the family home and not in a public area. There is evidence to show that permanent memorials at or near the location where someone died or went missing can have huge impact on vulnerable people who may be considering taking their own life, and lead to increased suicidal behaviour' (2018: 4).

7   Although Kposowa and McElvain write in the American context, their observations also pertain to the UK.

8   Robert Thompson's Craftsmen is a company based in Kilburn, Yorkshire, which makes wooden furniture in the Arts and Crafts tradition. The workshop was founded by Robert 'Mouseman' Thompson (1876–1955), and each piece carries the signature carved mouse symbol for which he became famous.

9   *Another Place* was originally conceived for a site on the mudflats outside Cuxhaven in Germany, which holds a similar proximity to the industrial port of Hamburg. The sculptures were installed at Crosby in 2005, and the decision to make the installation permanent followed in 2007.

10 An extensive programme of renovation for Gormley's installation at Crosby beach began in 2019 with a focus on rectifying the leaning figures by renewing their foundations.

11 In a subsequent clarification of continuing bonds, Klass cautioned against mistaking a 'description' for a 'prescription' (2006: 844). The intention of the new model, he pointed out, was not to replace the 'harmful' with the 'helpful' (2006: 845) but 'to show that interacting with the dead could be normal rather than pathological' (2006: 844).

12 Although Facebook and other online platforms can provide valuable repositories for memories of the deceased, Bailey et al. have cautioned that potential pitfalls for the bereaved include 'changes to the site without their consent' and 'removal of the page without their consent' (2015: 84).

Figure 5 My sister, the Stray, Redcar, 1988. Photograph © the author

CODA
WHO?

This book has argued that the relation of suicide emerges out of the entanglement of people, things, practices and discourses. Not only this, but the entanglement of these various agencies is *productive* of suicide, in that it underpins how suicide both materializes and comes to matter in our everyday lives. Relating suicide refers in this study not only to the narration of a pre-existing event but also to the ways in which that act of relation shapes how suicide is constructed and understood. I have intertwined my own experience of losing my sister to suicide with others' representations of suicide to create a diverse community of voices that speak with, through and at times across and aslant each other, and that together convey something of the contingent and messy business of what it means to relate suicide. In lieu of a conclusion, which would belie the necessarily incomplete and ongoing nature of relating suicide, I follow Donna Haraway's lead in '[s]taying with the trouble' (2016: 1), which is to recognize that suicide is 'inextricably entwined in myriad unfinished configurations of places, times, matters, meanings' (2016: 1).

This coda takes up the question of who, which has run through the preceding chapters without being explicitly addressed. It does so in the belief that change is, in the words of Carolyn Pedwell, 'not a faraway destination on the horizon but is continually unfolding in the present through the evolving interactions between organisms and their milieus' (2021: 147). Transformation thus lies in attending to the potentialities that are immanent, but not yet fully realized, in the present. I also pose the question in the light of Jennifer White's observation that the relationality of suicide 'includes reckoning with the fact that we are always living and working in the midst of interlocking systems, structures and discourses that both (re-)produce harm and also shape understandings of what it means to be human and live a worthwhile life' (2020: 197). White reminds us that attention to the present should be alert not only to emerging formations of care but also to our own complicity in the institutions and structures that can contribute to rendering some lives unliveable. In what follows, I reflect on who is entangled in the relationalities through which suicide is materialized in the contemporary (and who is not). In the words of Eva Haifa Giraud, are there 'entities, practices, and ways of being that are *foreclosed* when ... entangled realities are materialized' (2019: 2)? If so, can we pull out of the pages of this book some threads that might help us to generate and inhabit different forms of community and relationality in suicide's wake?

The first thread that I want to pluck out of the chapters is the question of who is counted in the category of suicide: focused on the completed act, the term disconnects suicide from those who either intend to commit suicide and change their minds or who have survived a suicide attempt. The current configuration of suicide, in other words, perpetuates the historical separation of *suicide* as a legal category and *suicidal* as a medical or psychiatric diagnosis. I noted in Chapter 1 that the suicidal are typically approached as objects of care rather than as thinking, feeling, adaptable agents. Staying with the trouble of suicide entails asking how we might better attend to the relation of suicide by the suicidal. Katrina Jaworski has called for a new attitude of 'wonder and generosity' in suicide research, which would entail 'recognizing the needs of those who survived suicide' in a way that acknowledges difference (2020b: 595). How, Jaworski asks, *do* we listen to the stories of those who have survived a suicide attempt? She solicits the researcher to adopt a stance of humility: '[t]his kind of listening means that we respect th[e] choices [of the suicidal] as their own, based on the meaning *they* attribute to it' (2020b: 596). Valuing the knowledge of those who have survived suicide necessitates putting aside our own frameworks, including 'clinical categor[ies]' (2020b: 596) and foregrounding the relational as an ethical stance. Amy Chandler has also taken up this question with reference to the integration of the lived experience of suicidality into qualitative research. She argues that 'it is vital that accounts are analysed and presented critically, theorised and tied to broader issues of justice, inequality and oppression' (2020b: 39). Here, too, relationality plays a central role in connecting the knowledge of those who have experienced suicidal thoughts or attempted suicide to wider socio-political contexts and asking how they in turn shape individual feelings and actions.

Beyond the academy, the National Suicide Prevention Alliance (NPSA) has played a vital role in integrating the lived experience of suicide into suicide prevention in the UK context. In 2011, the Samaritans, in partnership with the Department of Health, launched 'A Call to Action for Suicide Prevention', which aimed to join up organizations and agencies across sectors. The 'Call to Action Declaration', which followed in 2012, was launched in conjunction with the government's new National Suicide Prevention Strategy. The alliance of organizations that the Declaration represented evolved into the NPSA, which was formally constituted in 2013. Core to the work of the NPSA is the belief that everyone, including those with lived experience of suicide, has an important role to play in reducing the incidence of suicide. The Lived Experience Network ensures that the NPSA's suicide prevention strategy is underpinned by the knowledge of those who have experienced suicidal thoughts and/or attempted suicide, as well as by their families and those who have been bereaved by suicide. The NPSA's entangling of lived experience, in all its diversity, into the materialization of knowledge about suicide offers a valuable model for countering the foreclosure of knowledges and ways of being in addressing suicide and a demonstration of how change can be meaningfully enacted in the present through emerging and shifting formations.

The second thread I want to pick up is the experiences of those who have been bereaved by suicide. In Chapter 2, I considered that a death by suicide often entails an entanglement for those left behind with coronial procedures. Experiences of inquest proceedings vary considerably across and even within families, and their relation is necessarily multiple and contradictory. This book has positioned coronial procedure as a network of people, bodies and practices in and through which suicide is materialized (or not). The dead body becomes entangled with a variety of documents and discourses – including, but not limited to, the pathologist's report, medical photographs of the autopsy, coronial law, and medical and psychiatric records – which together constitute the forms of knowledge that shape how suicide is publicly related and/or named. The testimony of the bereaved is knotted into this tangle, but their knowledge can too often be experienced as marginalized when the death is related in the courtroom at the close of coronial proceedings, and/or as it is subsequently recorded on the death certificate. The secondary importance accorded to the experiences of the bereaved troubles, in Haraway's terms, who the coroner's court is, or should be, responsible to – the living or the dead. Historically, the court's function is to investigate an undetermined cause of death, but, in cases of suspected suicide, might it more adequately address the needs of the bereaved in the present? Stefan Timmermans has posed the central question as follows: '[W]ho has the ability to make authoritative suicide judgements: relatives who knew the deceased intimately, or professionals who impute intentions?' (2006: 76).

Chapter 2 outlined the recent change in the coronial law of England and Wales to the civil standard of evidence, which should result in a more accurate counting of suicide by producing less open-verdict outcomes. The Coroners and Justice Act of 2009 also introduced a welcome series of reforms into coronial procedure in England and Wales, which relate directly to how the bereaved encounter and experience the coronial process. The Act should help to mitigate some of the more negative effects of the coronial system on the bereaved. According to the Chief Coroner's Guide, the Act sought to standardize practice with the introduction of a Chief Coroner to oversee procedures and appointments. Reforms also addressed concerns relating to stigmatization. Language that implied criminalization was removed or revised: the word 'inquisition' was deemed 'inappropriate', while 'verdicts' were now to be referred to as 'conclusions' (2013: 22). A jury might only be summoned under limited circumstances. A new regulation allowed coroners to delegate administrative duties, including contacting bereaved relatives, to 'their officers and other support staff' (2013: 7). The post-mortem was purposefully 'expressed in such a way that it can include … forms of examination other than the … autopsy' (2013: 11), meaning that the results of less invasive procedures – for example, an MRI or CT scan – can be used where appropriate. Together, these changes comprise an overdue modernization and regularization of coronial procedure in England and Wales. Nevertheless, the public nature of the proceedings was maintained, if not reinforced, by the Act in the interests of 'transparency in the coronial process' (2013: 16). This aspect of the hearings will need to be balanced carefully against the emotional needs and sensitivities of the bereaved. Although the Act set out new rights of appeal against decisions of coroners, these were subsequently repealed in 2011. Chapple et al. rightly caution that greater input of the bereaved in coronial outcomes might mean that 'concordance [is] hard to achieve if coroners and families use different and contradictory evidence' (2012: 236). Even so, the family's knowledge of the deceased might be registered with greater sensitivity as standard practice in the coronial hearing. Throughout this book, I have located meaningful change in the everyday habits and routines that allow new modes of social and institutional life to take shape. Attending to how the rituals, gestures and spaces of the coroner's court affect the bereaved, as well as familiarizing relatives with the courtroom and its procedures in advance of a hearing, would accordingly also constitute a positive ongoing praxis that might help to transform the lived encounter between the bereaved and the coronial structure.

Countering the solitariness of the suicidal act, this book has focused on how suicide ripples out among the living through acts of telling and narration. In Chapter 3, I proposed that relating suicide expands kinship around and in relation to the dead so that new lines of connection and responsibility can be forged. Elaborating on the expansion of care to those who are not (yet) known, the Care Collective observe:

> While care for strangers may seem a hard emotion to cultivate, developing a comfort with the foreign or alien is not actually beyond us. Forms of everyday cosmopolitanism emerge quite spontaneously in the lives of cities, where people historically considered strangers to one another intermingle and combine in the course of their daily lives. ... Being cosmopolitan means being at ease with strangeness; knowing that we have no choice but to live with difference, whatever differences come to matter in specific times and places.
>
> (2020: 95)

I am struck, reading this passage, by the specifically metropolitan imaginary that is at work.[1] The sociality of suicide, as it has been imagined in the creative and critical texts considered in this book, is likewise (con)figured in urban settings. It has registered in the chimes of Big Ben and the foggy atmospheres over London. The River Foyle running through the heart of Derry-Londonderry has constellated questions of division and connection, of how to live beside one another even as suicide demands new forms of relationality. Jocelyn Lim Chua's ethnographic study of suicide is situated in the capital city of Kerala and the relational networks that she traces are embedded in the institutional and neighbourhood infrastructures of the metropole. The third thread I want to pull out is therefore the marginalization of those who live beyond or outside the city in suicide's current configurations. Staying with the trouble of suicide entails disrupting the centrality accorded to metropolitan experience and imagining how suicide prevention might be woven into the everyday across a more diverse range of places, landscapes and communities. The ongoing project is to build and sustain networks of care in rural, coastal and/or island locations.[2]

Suicide has emerged in this book as a pervasive and routine presence in our everyday lives. Its very familiarity means that it can be overlooked: it is hidden in plain sight all around us. It appears and disappears in verdicts, wooden benches, Facebook pages and clichés. I have understood suicide as a phenomenon that we *all* live with, albeit with varying degrees of kinship.

Chua has remarked that the stories about suicide that she encountered in her research 'were not windows onto an event, narrowly defined, as much as they were openings onto the ways in which individuals and loved ones laboured to make meaning in the wake of death' (2014: 23). I have similarly focused on how suicide takes shape among the living, drawing on my own and others' experience of the weeks, months and years following a death by suicide. I have sought throughout this book to bring to attention not only the proximity of suicide but also the practicalities that follow in its wake. Although I have followed a broadly chronological timeframe through the chapters, suicide's aftermath does not lend itself to any easy resolution or closure. We are repeatedly urged to talk more about suicide in order to challenge and break down the silence and stigma that continue to surround the subject. It is equally important, I propose, that we listen more, too. This means listening to a greater diversity of voices so that we include in the production of knowledge about suicide those who have, in various ways, lived in closest proximity to it. It means listening *beyond* what is spoken, remaining alert to the affective currents that pulsate in and through our everyday encounters, as well as to the multiple ways in which institutional, social, economic and cultural environments shape what is being said. It also means registering, and making accommodation for, the gaps and silences that delineate what we do not – and cannot – know about suicide: the knowledge that ultimately belongs to the dead alone. This does not mean that suicide is unsayable; it is, to return to Denise Riley's suggestive formulation, 'at least … half tellable' ([2012] 2019: 19). It is to recognize, rather, that the act is caught between the known and the unknown, the spoken and the unspoken, and to live, work and write, from within the complex relationalities that this affords.

Notes

1   Examples of care spaces in *The Care Manifesto* are likewise metropolitan. See, for example, the discussion of the funding of the Southbank Centre by the Greater London Council as central to a range of initiatives designed to support accessibility and to help 'democratise intellectual and cultural activity across London' (2020: 49).

2   The Farming Community Network provides support for farmers in the UK, a profession that experiences high suicide rates. Suicide in rural areas is typically framed in relation to farming, and it is worth asking whether this potentially obscures other populations in rural communities who may also be vulnerable to suicide.

BIBLIOGRAPHY

Adorján, Johanna ([2009] 2012), *An Exclusive Love: A Memoir*, trans. by Anthea
   Bell, London: Vintage.
Ahmed, Sara (2004), *The Cultural Politics of Emotion*, Edinburgh: Edinburgh
   University Press.
Ahmed, Sara (2006a), 'Orientations: Toward a Queer Phenomenology', *GLQ:
   A Journal of Lesbian and Gay Studies*, 12 (4): 543–74.
Ahmed, Sara (2006b), *Queer Phenomenology: Orientations, Objects, Others*,
   Durham and London: Duke University Press.
Ahmed, Sara (2010), *The Promise of Happiness*, Durham and London: Duke
   University Press.
Anderson, Darran (2020), *Inventory: A River, a City, a Family*, London: Chatto and
   Windus.
Bailey, Louis, Jo Bell and David Kennedy (2015), 'Continuing Social Presence of
   the Dead: Exploring Suicide Bereavement through Online Memorialisation',
   New Review of Hypermedia and Multimedia, 21 (1–2): 72–86.
Balayannis, Angeliki and Brian Robert Cook (2016), 'Suicide at a Distance: The
   Paradox of Knowing Self-Destruction', *Progress in Human Geography*, 40 (4):
   530–45.
Bambra, Clare and Joanne Cairns (2017), 'The Impact of Place on Suicidal
   Behaviour', *Socioeconomic Disadvantage and Suicidal Behaviour Report*,
   The Samaritans, 8–31. https://media.samaritans.org/documents/
   Socioeconomic_disadvantage_and_suicidal_behaviour_-_Full.pdf
Baraitser, Lisa (2020), 'Denise Riley and Lisa Baraitser in Conversation', *Feminist
   Theory*, 21 (3): 339–49.
Beaumont, Matthew (2012), 'Beginnings, Endings, Births, Deaths: Sterne, Dickens,
   and *Bleak House*', *Textual Practice*, 26 (5): 807–27.
Bell, Jo, Louis Bailey and David Kennedy (2015), '"We Do It to Keep Him Alive":
   Bereaved Individuals' Experiences of Online Suicide Memorials and Continuing
   Bonds', *Mortality*, 20 (4): 375–89.
Bell, Vikki (2020), '"Always Another Breath on My Breath": On Denise Riley, the
   Polyvocality of the Subject and Poetry', *Feminist Theory*, 21 (3): 317–29.
Bennett, Andrew (2017), *Suicide Century: Literature and Suicide from James Joyce to
   David Foster Wallace*, Cambridge: Cambridge University Press.
Berman, Jeffrey (1999), *Surviving Literary Suicide*, Minneapolis: University of
   Minnesota Press.
Biddle, Lucy (2003), 'Public Hazards or Private Tragedies? An Exploratory Study of
   the Effect of Coroners' Procedures on Those Bereaved by Suicide', *Social Science
   and Medicine*, 56 (5): 1033–45.

Bibliography

Biss, Eula (2012), 'The Pain Scale', www.sureview.org.biss.pdf.

Bloomfield, Mandy (2016), *Archaeopoetics: Word, Image, History*, Tuscaloosa: University of Alabama Press.

Bourke, Joanna (2014), *The Story of Pain: From Prayer to Painkillers*, Oxford: Oxford University Press.

Butler, Judith (2004), *Precarious Life: The Powers of Mourning and Violence*, London and New York: Verso.

Butler, Judith (2015), *Notes Toward a Performative Theory of Assembly*, Cambridge and London: Harvard University Press.

Butler, Judith (2020), 'Time "Is" the Person: An Essay on *Time Lived, without Its Flow* (Riley, 2012)', *Feminist Theory*, 21 (3): 331–7.

Button, Mark E. (2016), 'Suicide and Social Justice: Toward a Political Approach to Suicide', *Political Research Quarterly* 69 (2): 270–80.

Button, Mark E. and Ian Marsh, eds. (2019), *Suicide and Social Justice: New Perspectives on the Politics of Suicide and Suicide Prevention*, London and New York: Routledge.

Care Collective, The (2020), *The Care Manifesto: The Politics of Interdependence*, London and New York: Verso.

Caroline Flack: Her Life and Death (2021), [TV documentary], dir. Charlie Russell, Channel 4, 17 March.

Carruthers, Jo and Nour Dakkuk (2020), 'Introduction: Sandscapes', in Jo Carruthers and Nour Dakkak (eds.), *Sandscapes: Writing the British Seaside*, 1–18, Basingstoke: Palgrave.

Cavarero, Adriana (2016), *Inclinations: A Critique of Rectitude*, trans. by Amanda Minervini, Stanford: Stanford University Press.

Chandler, Amy (2020), 'Shame as Affective Injustice: Qualitative, Sociological Explorations of Self-Harm, Suicide and Socio-economic Inequalities', in Mark E. Button and Ian Marsh (eds.), *Suicide and Social Justice: New Perspectives on the Politics of Suicide and Suicide Prevention*, 32–49, London and New York: Routledge.

Chapple, Alison, Sue Ziebland and Keith Hawton (2012), 'A Proper, Fitting Explanation? Suicide Bereavement and Perceptions of the Coroner's Verdict', *Crisis: The Journal of Crisis Intervention and Suicide Prevention*, 33: 230–8.

Chief Coroner (2013), 'The Chief Coroner's Guide to the Coroners and Justice Act 2009', https://www.judiciary.uk/wp-content/uploads/JCO/Documents/coroners/guidance/chief-coroners-guide-to-act-Sept2013.pdf

Chua, Jocelyn Lim (2014), *In Search of the Good Life: Aspiration and Suicide in Globalizing South India*, Berkeley: University of California Press.

Clark, Sheila E. and Robert D. Goldney (2000), 'The Impact of Suicide on Relatives and Friends', in Keith Hawton and Kees van Heeringen (eds.), *The International Handbook of Suicide and Attempted Suicide*, 1–6, Chichester: John Wiley.

Connor, Steven (2010), 'The Dust That Measures All Our Time', http://stevenconnor.com/sand/

Critchley, Simon (2015), *Notes on Suicide*, London: Fitzcarraldo.

Cvetkovich, Ann (2003), *An Archive of Feelings: Trauma, Sexuality, and Lesbian Public Cultures*, Durham and London: Duke University Press.

DeNora, Tia (2014), *Making Sense of Reality: Culture and Perception in Everyday Life*, London: Sage.

Dickens, Charles ([1852–53] 2008), *Bleak House*, ed. and with an Introduction and Notes by Stephen Gill, Oxford: Oxford University Press.

DocHouse (2018), '*Evelyn*: Director Q & A', Carol Nahta in Conversation with Orlando von Einsiedel, Gwendolyn von Einsiedel, and Joanna Natsegara, 3 December, www.dochouse.org.

Dorling, Danny and David Gunnell (2003), 'Suicide: The Spatial and Social Components of Despair in Britain 1980–2000', *Transactions – Institute of British Geographers*, 28 (4): 442–60.

Doughty, Louise (2019), *Platform Seven*, London: Faber.

Evelyn (2018), Dir. Orlando von Einsiedel, London: Grain Media and Violet Films.

Felski, Rita (2000), *Doing Time: Feminist Theory and Postmodern Culture*, New York: New York University Press.

Frank, Arthur (1995), *The Wounded Storyteller: Body, Illness, and Ethics*, Chicago: University of Chicago Press.

Giraud, Eva Haifa (2019), *What Comes after Entanglement? Activism, Anthropocentrism, and an Ethics of Exclusion*, Durham and London: Duke University Press.

Glendenning, Victoria (2006), *Leonard Woolf: A Biography*, New York: Simon & Schuster.

Grosz, Elizabeth (2004), *The Nick of Time: Politics, Evolution, and the Untimely*, Durham and London: Duke University Press.

Handke, Peter ([1972] 2012), *A Sorrow beyond Dreams: A Life Story*, trans. by Ralph Mannheim, introd. by Jeffrey Eugenides, New York: Farrar, Straus and Giroux.

Haraway, Donna (2016), *Staying with the Trouble: Making Kin in the Chthulucene*, Durham and London: Duke University Press.

Harpin, Anna (2018), *Madness, Art and Society: Beyond Illness*, Abingdon: Routledge.

Ingold, Tim (2015), *The Life of Lines*, Abingdon: Routledge.

Jamison, Kay Redfield (1999), *Night Falls Fast: Understanding Suicide*, New York: Picador.

Jansson, Asa (2013), 'From Statistics to Diagnostics: Medical Certificates, Melancholia, and "Suicidal Propensities" in Victorian Psychiatry', *Journal of Social History*, 46 (3): 716–31.

Jaworski, Katrina (2010), 'The Author, Agency and Suicide', *Social Identities* 16 (5): 675–87.

Jaworski, Katrina (2014), *The Gender of Suicide: Knowledge Production, Theory and Suicidology*, London and New York: Routledge.

Jaworski, Katrina (2015), 'Suicide, Agency and the Limits of Power', in Ludek Broz and Daniel Münster (eds.), *Suicide and Agency: Anthropological Perspectives on Self-Destruction, Personhood, and Power*, 183–201, London and New York: Routledge.

Jaworski, Katrina (2020a), 'A Longing to Be Heard as the Longing to Die Lingers: An Afterword', in Daniel G. Scott (ed.), *Voicing Suicide*, 163–84, Victoria, British Columbia: Ekstasis Editions.

Jaworski, Katrina (2020b), 'Towards an Ethics of Wonder and Generosity in Critical Suicidology', *Social Epistemology*, 34 (6): 589–600.

Jaworski, Katrina and Daniel G. Scott (2016), 'Understanding the Unfathomable in Suicide: Poetry, Absence, and the Corporeal Body', in Jennifer White, Ian Marsh, Michael J. Kral and Jonathan Morris (eds.), *Critical Suicidology: Transforming*

Suicide Research and Prevention for the 21st Century, 209–28, Vancouver and Toronto: University of British Columbia Press.

Jaworski, Katrina and Daniel G. Scott (2020), 'At the Limits of Suicide: The Bad Timing of the Gift', *Social Epistemology*, 34 (6): 577–88.

Jennings, Elizabeth (2012), *The Collected Poems*, ed. by Emma Mason, Manchester: Carcanet.

Jordan, Ana and Amy Chandler (2019), 'Crisis, What Crisis? A Feminist Analysis of Discourse on Masculinities and Suicide', *Journal of Gender Studies* 28 (4): 462–74.

Kellaher, Leonie and Ken Warpole (2010), 'Bringing the Dead Back Home: Urban Spaces as Sites for New Patterns of Mourning and Remembrance', in Avril Maddrell and James D. Sidaway (eds.), *Deathscapes: Spaces for Death, Dying, Mourning and Remembrance*, 179–98, London: Taylor and Francis.

Klass, Dennis (2006), 'Continuing Conversation about Continuing Bonds', *Death Studies*, 30: 843–58.

Klass, Dennis, Phyllis R. Silverman, and Steven L. Nickman, eds. (1996), *Continuing Bonds: New Understandings of Grief*, New York and London: Routledge.

Kposowa, Augustine J. and James P. McElvain (2020), 'Gender, Place, and Method of Suicide', *Social Psychiatry and Psychiatric Epidemiology*, 41 (6): 435–43.

Kryskinska, Karolina and Karl Andriessen (2015), 'Online Memorialization and Grief after Suicide', *OMEGA – Journal of Death and Dying*, 71 (1): 19–47.

Laing, Olivia (2012), *To the River: A Journey Beneath the Surface*, Edinburgh: Canongate.

Levine, Caroline (2015), *Forms: Whole, Rhythm, Hierarchy, Network*, Princeton: Princeton University Press.

Li, Yiyun (2019), *Where Reasons End: A Novel*, London: Hamish Hamilton.

Limburg, Joanne (2017a), *The Autistic Alice*, Hexham: Bloodaxe.

Limburg, Joanna (2017b), *Small Pieces: A Book of Lamentations*, London: Atlantic Books.

Maddrell, Avril (2012), 'Online Memorials: The Virtual as the New Vernacular', *Bereavement Care*, 31 (2): 46–54.

Maddrell, Avril (2013), 'Living with the Deceased: Absence, Presence and Absence-Presence', *Cultural Geographies*, 20 (4): 501–22.

Maddrell, Avril (2016), 'Mapping Grief: A Conceptual Framework for Understanding the Spatial Dimensions of Bereavement, Mourning and Remembrance', *Social and Cultural Geography*, 17 (2): 166–88.

Manguso, Sarah (2012), *The Guardians: An Elegy*, London: Granta.

Marsh, Ian (2010), *Suicide: Foucault, History and Truth*, Cambridge: Cambridge University Press.

Millard, Chris (2015), *A History of Self-Harm in Britain: A Genealogy of Cutting and Overdosing*, Basingstoke: Palgrave.

Mills, China (2020), 'Strengthening Borders and Toughening Up on Welfare: Death by Suicide in the UK's Hostile Environment', in Mark E. Button and Ian Marsh (eds.), *Suicide and Social Justice: New Perspectives on the Politics of Suicide and Suicide Prevention*, 71–86, London and New York: Routledge.

Morrissey, Sinéad (2019), 'Put Off That Mask: Trauma, Persona and Authenticity in Denise Riley's "A Part Song"', *PN Review*, 250: 19–23.

Network Rail (2021), 'Fatalities', https://www.networkrail.co.uk/running-the-railway/looking-after-the-railway/delays-explained/fatalities/

Newby, Diana Rose (2020), 'Bleak Environmentalism: The Science of Dickens's Weathered Bodies', *Texas Studies in Literature and Language*, 62 (2): 178–202.

Ní Dochartaigh, Kerri (2021), *Thin Places*, Edinburgh: Canongate.

Nixon, Rob (2013), *Slow Violence and the Environmentalism of the Poor*, Cambridge, MA: Harvard University Press.

Olson, Liesl (2003), 'Virginia Woolf's "Cotton Wool of Daily Life"', *Journal of Modern Literature*, 26 (2): 42–65.

Outka, Elizabeth (2020), *Viral Modernism: The Influenza Pandemic and Interwar Literature*, New York: Columbia University Press.

Pedwell, Carolyn (2021), *Revolutionary Routines: The Habits of Social Transformation*, Montreal, London and Chicago: McGill-Queen's University Press.

Pedwell, Carolyn, and Anne Whitehead (2012), 'Introduction: Affecting Feminism: Questions of Feeling in Feminist Theory', *Feminist Theory* 13 (2): 115–29.

Pollock, Griselda (2018), *Charlotte Salomon and the Theatre of Memory*, New Haven and London: Yale University Press.

Puar, Jasbir K. (2011), 'Coda: The Cost of Getting Better: Suicide, Sensation, Switchpoints', *GLQ: A Journal of Lesbian and Gay Studies*, 18 (1): 149–58.

Public Health Agency of Northern Ireland (2018), *Advice for Families on Public Memorials Following a Sudden Death That Is a Suspected Suicide*, https://www.publichealth.hscni.net

Randall, Bryony (2007), *Modernism, Daily Time and Everyday Life*, Cambridge: Cambridge University Press.

Riley, Denise (2005), *Impersonal Passion: Language as Affect*, Durham and London: Duke University Press.

Riley, Denise (2016), *Say Something Back*, London: Picador.

Riley, Denise ([2012] 2019) *Time Lived, without Its Flow*, introd. by Max Porter, London: Picador.

Salisbury, Laura (2016), 'Aphasic Modernism: Languages for Illness from a Confusion of Tongues', in Anne Whitehead, Angela Woods, Sarah Atkinson, Jane Macnaughton and Jennifer Richards (eds.), *Edinburgh Companion to the Critical Medical Humanities*, 444–62, Edinburgh: Edinburgh University Press.

Salmela, Anu (2018), 'Fleshy Stories: New Materialism and Female Suicides in Late Nineteenth-Century Finland', *International Journal for History, Culture and Modernity*, 6 (1): 1–27.

Scarry, Elaine (1985), *The Body in Pain: The Making and Unmaking of the World*, New York and Oxford: Oxford University Press.

Sharpe, Christina (2016), *In the Wake: On Blackness and Being*, Durham and London: Duke University Press.

Shildrick, Margaret (2015), 'Living On; Not Getting Better', *Feminist Review*, 111 (2015): 10–24.

Stepanova, Maria (2021), *In Memory of Memory: A Romance*, trans. by Sasha Dugdale, London: Fitzcarraldo.

Bibliography

Stevenson, Lisa (2014), *Life Beside Itself: Imagining Care in the Canadian Arctic*, Oakland: University of California Press.

Stevenson, Olivia (2016), 'Suicidal Journeys: Attempted Suicide as Geographies of Intended Death', *Social and Cultural Geography*, 17 (2): 189–206.

Stewart, Kathleen (2007), *Ordinary Affects*, Durham and London: Duke University Press.

Szirtes, George (2019), *The Photographer at Sixteen*, London: MacLehose.

Tack, Saartje (2019), 'The Logic of Life: Suicide through Somatechnics', *Australian Feminist Studies*, 34 (99): 46–59.

Timmermans, Stefan (2006), *Postmortem: How Medical Examiners Explain Suspicious Deaths*, Chicago and London: University of Chicago Press.

Turnbull, Pauline, Louis Appleby, Nev Kapur, David Gunnell and Keith Hawton (2019), 'New Standard of Proof for Suicides at Inquests in England and Wales', *British Medical Journal*, 366, 29 July, https://doi.org/10.1136/bmj.14745

Warren, Jonathan (2018), *Industrial Teesside, Lives and Legacies: A Post-Industrial Geography*, Basingstoke: Palgrave Macmillan.

Wertheimer, Alison (2014), *A Special Scar: The Experiences of People Bereaved by Suicide*, 3rd Edition, London and New York: Routledge.

White, Jennifer (2020), 'Hello Cruel World! Embracing a Collective Ethics for Suicide Prevention', in Mark E. Button and Ian Marsh (eds.), *Suicide and Social Justice: New Perspectives on the Politics of Suicide and Suicide Prevention*, 197–210, London and New York: Routledge.

White, Jennifer, Ian Marsh, Michael J. Kral, and Jonathan Morris (2016), 'Introduction: Rethinking Suicide', in Jennifer White, Ian Marsh, Michael J. Kral and Jonathan Morris (eds.), *Critical Suicidology: Transforming Suicide Research and Prevention for the Twenty-First Century*, 1–12, Vancouver: University of British Columbia Press.

Whitehead, Anne and Angela Woods (2016), 'Introduction', in Anne Whitehead, Angela Woods, Sarah Atkinson, Jane Macnaughton and Jennifer Richards (eds.), *The Edinburgh Companion to the Critical Medical Humanities*, 1–31, Edinburgh: Edinburgh University Press.

Woods, Angela (2012), 'Beyond the Wounded Storyteller: Rethinking Illness, Narrativity, and Embodied Self-Experience', in Havi Carel and Rachel Cooper (eds.), *Health, Illness, and Disease: Philosophical Perspectives*, 113–28, Newcastle: Acumen.

Woolf, Virginia ([1925] 1984), 'Modern Fiction', in Andrew McNeille (ed.), *Essays of Virginia Woolf*, Vol. 4: 1925–1928, 157–65, London: Hogarth Press.

Woolf, Virginia ([1925] 2000), *Mrs. Dalloway*, ed. by Stella McNichol, introd. by Elaine Showalter, Harmondsworth: Penguin.

Woolf, Virginia ([1930] 2012), *On Being Ill, with Notes from Sick Rooms*, introd. by Hermione Lee, afterword by Rita Charon, Ashfield: Paris Press.

INDEX

Locators followed by 'n.' indicate endnotes

Adorján, Johanna 23, 65 n.2
affective atmospheres 54–65, 75
Ahmed, Sara 8, 31, 85
  kitchen table as object 90, 93–4
  orientation 31–2, 37 n.7, 83
  shame 61
  sticky objects 8–10, 15–16, 22, 47–8, 93
  straightening device 85
American Pain Foundation 53
Anderson, Darran, *Inventory* 11, 49, 54,
    71–3, 94–5 n.3
  Andrew 73–4
  Anthony 72–3
  Budgie 72
  cracked barometer 72–3, 94
  DD's suicide 71–2
  Joseph 73
  River Foyle (Derry-Londonderry) 49,
    72–3, 75, 94 n.3
  slow violence 74
Andriessen, Karl 88

Bailey, Louis, online memorial practices
    88–9, 95 n.12
Balayannis, Angeliki 3
Bambra, Clare 70–1
Beaufort Scale 54
Beaumont, Matthew 58
Bell, Jo 87, 89
Bell, Vanessa 37 n.9, 65 n.6
Bell, Vikki 46
Bennett, Andrew 6, 8, 10, 30, 65 n.4
  pharmakon 7
  Suicide Century 7
  suicide memoirs 6–7
bereavement, suicide 3–4, 20, 36 n.1, 41–2,
    45–6, 48–9, 61–2, 69, 79–81, 83,
    86–9, 92–3, 95 n.12, 99–100
Berman, Jeffrey, *Surviving Literary Suicide* 7
Biddle, Lucy 54, 61–2
Biss, Eula, The Pain Scale 53–4
Bloody Sunday incident (1972) 72
Bloomfield, Mandy 43

body and autopsy 10, 29, 50–3, 62, 65 n.7, 100
  coroner orders 50
  family's identification 4, 10, 17, 49–50, 62
Boro Walkers Association (Teesside United
    campaign) 95 n.5
Bourke, Joanna 66 n.8
Burial of Suicides Act (1824) 54
Butler, Judith 36 n.2, 45–6, 77, 85
  grievable life 2
  theory of performativity 64
Button, Mark E. 74

Cairns, Joanne 70–1
Call to Action Declaration (National
    Suicide Prevention Strategy) 98–9
care
  in *The Care Manifesto* 101, 102 n.1
  communities of 86–94
  The Care Collective 92, 101
  The Care Manifesto (The Care Collective)
    92, 102 n.1
  Caroline Flack: Her Life and Death (Channel
    4 documentary) 81–2
Carruthers, Jo 86
Carstone, Richard 60
cause of death 35, 50–1, 55, 57, 88, 99
Cavarero, Adriana, relational ontology 85
Chandler, Amy 5, 74, 98
chaos narrative 6
Chapple, Alison 62–3, 100
Chua, Jocelyn Lim 69
  suicide ethnography (Kerala, India) 9,
    29, 101–2
civil standard of evidence 63–4, 100
Clark, Sheila E. 3
cliché-land, suicide as 10, 41–9, 65 n.4
  condolence letter 43
  language 10, 42, 45–6, 88
  tragedy 42
co-habitation/sharing of space 94
communities of care 86–94
compositional approach 71
Connor, Steven 86

Index

contemporary suicide research 37 n.4
contextual explanation 71
Cook, Brian Robert 3
Coronavirus pandemic 78
Coroners and Justice Act (2009) 100
coronial law/process 4–6, 22, 36, 37 n.10,
    50, 63–4
    Australian 5
    in *Bleak House* (Dickens) 10, 56–7, 60
    England and Wales 63, 100
    transparency in 100
Court of Appeal in England and Wales 63
Critchley, Simon 37 n.10
critical approaches 4, 8–9
critical suicidology 4–5, 37 n.7
    medical humanities 5–7, 11
Cross, Merry 66 n.10
cultural considerations of suicide 71
Cvetkovich, Ann 8
    archive of feelings 45, 83

Dakkak, Nour 86
death certificate 35, 80, 83, 99
DeNora, Tia 24
Dickens, Charles, *Bleak House* 8, 10
    Accidental Death 57
    atmosphere, role of 58, 64
    coronial law 10, 56–7, 60
    Dedlock, Leicester 59
    Inspector Bucket 57, 59
    Jarndyce & Jarndyce lawsuit 56–7, 60
    Lady Dedlock 56–7, 59–60
    Nemo and Krook 56–61
    sign of suicidal intention 59
    suicide and Chancery 56, 58, 60
    Tulkinghorn 57, 59–60
    Weevle and Guppy 56, 58, 60
Dorling, Danny 70
Doughty, Louise, *Platform Seven* 9, 78–81
drowning 4, 33, 35, 49–53, 59, 65 n.7
    in cliché 41–8
    Inventory (Anderson) 49, 54, 72–3,
        94 n.3
    Woolf 34
Durkheim, Émile 54

economic considerations of suicide 71
entanglement 4, 6, 11, 13 n.2, 57, 97, 99
ethnographic study of suicide

Canadian Inuit (Stevenson) 9–10, 21–2,
    29–30
Kerala, India (Chua) 9, 29, 101

Facebook 88–9, 95 n.12, 101
The Farming Community Network 102 n.2
Fatality Hotline 79
Felski, Rita 24–5
female suicides 50, 74
    methods 50–2, 63–4
feminine-attempted-passive 52
feminist theory 8–9
Foyle, River (place of suicide) 9, 49, 72–3,
    75–7, 94 n.1, 94 n.3, 101
Frank, Arthur 6

gendered norms 74–5
Giraud, Eva Haifa 98
Glendenning, Victoria 65 n.6
Goldney, Robert D. 3
Good Friday Agreement (1998) 69, 94 n.2
Gormley, Antony 85–6
    Another Place 11, 84, 95 n.9
    Crosby Beach, sandscape 85–6, 95 n.9,
        95 n.10
Greater London Council 102 n.1
grief process/grieving 3–5, 45–7, 69, 80,
    86–90, 94
grievable life 2
Grosz, Elizabeth 8, 10, 20–1, 31, 94 n.1. *See
    also* nick of/in time
Gunnell, David 70

Handke, Peter 41
    impersonal well-being 41, 47
    mother's suicide 41, 47
Haraway, Donna 2, 97, 99
Harpin, Anna 58
    Diagnostic and Statistical Manual 86–7
health and wellbeing, suicide considerations
    71
history, suicide considerations 71
Hunt Cliff (place of suicide) 70

infrastructure, suicide considerations 71
Ingold, Tim 58
inquest. *See* post-mortem and inquest
intentionality, suicidal 7, 10, 29, 37 n.10,
    51–2, 83

Lady Dedlock (*Bleak House*) 59–60
registration of 55

Jamison, Kay Redfield 10
Jansson, Asa 54–5
Jaworski, Katrina 4–5, 10, 17–18, 36, 37 n.3, 37 n.4, 57, 64, 74
bodily disfigurement 51–2
gendered norms 74
wonder and generosity 98
Jennings, Elizabeth, The Way of Words and Language 19–20
Jordan, Ana 5, 74
Joyce, James 30

Kellaher, Leonie 82. *See also* low-key form of contemporary memorialisation
Klass, Dennis 90, 95 n.11
Continuing Bonds: New Understandings of Grief 87
knowledge 3–4, 6, 98–9, 102
Kposowa, Augustine J. 80
Kryskinska, Karolina 88

Laing, Olivia 35
Brooks 34
To the River 10, 32–4
Lee, River (place of suicide) 76
Levine, Caroline 56–7, 60
Limburg, Joanne 48
Sister (poem) 48, 65 n.5
Small Pieces 48, 50
The Lived Experience Network 99
long dying 65
low-key form of contemporary memorialisation 82

Maddrell, Avril 69, 79, 81–2, 84–6, 88. *See also* vernacular memorials
male suicides 50, 74. *See also* female suicides
Manguso, Sarah 50
Marsh, Ian, *Suicide: Foucault, History and Truth* 4–5
materialization of suicide 2–4, 6, 9, 36, 38 n.12, 69, 83, 85, 87, 90, 95 n.3, 97–9
McElvain, James P. 80
memoirs, suicide 6–7, 10–11, 23, 44, 48, 50, 65 n.2, 69, 71–3, 76–7, 87

methods of suicide (women) 50–2, 63–4
Middlesbrough, UK (place of suicide) 70, 77
Millard, Chris, organised and systematic source 55–6
Mills, China 5, 55, 95 n.4
Morrissey, Sinéad 47
Mrs. Dalloway (Woolf) 8, 10, 25–30, 33
Dr Bradshaw 26–7, 29, 33
Clarissa Dalloway 25–9, 37, 61
influenza pandemic 27–9, 37 n.5, 37 n.6
Rezia 28–9, 33
Septimus Smith's suicide 25–9, 33, 37 n.6, 52, 59
mythologization 49

Natasegara, Joanna 91
National Office for Statistics 63
National Suicide Prevention Alliance (NPSA) 98–9
National Trust 70
Newby, Diana Rose 58, 60
news of suicide 2, 4, 17–18, 26, 28–9, 41, 61, 89
nick of/in time 8, 10, 20–1, 30–6, 44, 76, 94 n.1
ní Dochartaigh, Kerri, *Thin Places* 11, 71, 75–8, 94 n.1, 95 n.4
Nikolai (*Where Reasons End*, Yiyun Li) 42–4, 47
Nixon, Rob 64, 70
No Substitute campaign (Redcar and Cleveland Borough Council) 95 n.5

Olson, Liesl 27–8
online suicide memorial platform 87–9, 95 n.12
orientation 31–2, 37 n.7, 83, 94
O'Sullivan, Michael 55
Ouse, River (place of suicide) 9, 32, 34–5, 48
Outka, Elizabeth 29, 37 n.6

pain/pain scale 21, 48–54, 65–6 n.8
Pedwell, Carolyn 8, 11, 97
Peterborough Railway Station (place of suicide) 9, 78–81
physical considerations of suicide 71
places of suicide 9, 11, 35, 80
Foyle (River, Derry-Londonderry) 9, 49, 72–3, 75–7, 94 n.1, 94 n.3, 101

Index

grief/death and 69, 78
Hunt Cliff 70
Lee, River (Cork) 76
Middlesbrough (UK) 70, 77
Ouse (River, Sussex) 9, 32, 34–5, 48
Peterborough Railway Station 9, 78–81
Stray (Redcar) xii, 2, 30, 35, 40, 43, 69,
    78, 83–4, 96
Plath, Sylvia 34
political considerations of suicide 71
Pollock, Griselda 38 n.11
post-mortem and inquest 4, 10, 49–51, 53,
    62–3, 65 n.7, 99–100
    anachronism 54–5
    Bleak House 56–8, 61
prevention, suicide 4–5, 31, 37 n.7, 70, 74,
    98–9, 101
promiscuous care 92
Puar, Jasbir K. 65
Public Health Agency for Northern Ireland
    95 n.6
public memorial 95 n.6

quest narrative 6

Randall, Bryony 24–6
rates, suicide 70–1, 102 n.2
    Derry-Londonderry (Northern Ireland)
        69, 71–2
    England and Wales 71
    Kerala (India) 29
    Middlesbrough (UK) 70
    Scotland 70–1
Redcar and Cleveland Borough Council
    95 n.5
relationality of suicide 2–4, 9, 69, 87, 97–8,
    101
Riley, Denise 10, 20, 36 n.1, 45, 51, 102
    arrested time 18, 20
    maternal loss 36 n.1
    A Part Song 46–7, 65 n.3
    Say Something Back 65 n.3
    temporalities 18–19
    Time Lived 36 n.2, 46

Sackville-West, Vita 65 n.6
Salisbury, Laura 8, 13 n.2
Salmela, Anu 65 n.7, 74
Salomon, Charlotte, *Life? Or Theatre?*
    38 n.11
Samaritans app 2, 70, 98

A Call to Action for Suicide Prevention 98
    donation 1–2
Scarry, Elaine 65 n.8
Scott, Daniel G. 17–18, 37 n.3, 37 n.4
self-destruction/murder 3, 54–5
self-infliction 52
Shakespeare, William, *The Tempest* 47
shame 61–2
Sharpe, Christina, wake work 12, 13 n.4
Shildrick, Margrit 66 n.10
site of death 81, 84. *See also* places of
    suicide
slow deaths 65
slow violence 64, 70, 74
social and economic deprivation 70
social and environmental factors 64–5
social causes, suicide 54
social-media sites 88–9
social scientists and health geographers 70–1
sociological/demographic mapping 11, 69,
    74, 86
statistics 54, 56, 63
Stepanova, Maria 38 n.11
Stevenson, Lisa 79
    suicide ethnography (Canadian Inuit)
        9–10, 21–2, 29–30
Stevenson, Olivia 10, 31
    suicidal journey 31–2, 35
Stewart, Kathleen, ordinary affect 8, 22–3,
    82–3, 89
sticky objects 8–9, 15–17, 47–8, 93
    alarm clock 21–2
stigma and criminalisation 61
stopped watch 14, 15–23, 35
Stray, Redcar (place of suicide) xii, 2, 30, 35,
    40, 43, 69, 78, 83–4, 96
suicidal journey 10, 31–3, 35–6, 38 n.11
suicide/suicidal 1, 54–55, 58, 97–8, 101
    category of 98
    considerations 71 (*see also specific
        considerations of suicide*)
    and day 23–6
    disturbance/disruption of time 17–18
    living beside 15
    materialization (*see* materialization of
        suicide)
    partial, indirect, and relational 3
    in rural areas 102 n.2
    sociality of 101
    and socio-economic deprivation 11
    telos/teleology 6, 10, 44

Suicide Act (1961) 54, 63, 66 n.9
suicide-prevention charities 63
suicidology 4, 37 n.7. *See also* critical
    suicidology
Survivors of Bereavement by Suicide 48
Szirtes, George, *The Photographer at Sixteen*
    44, 65 n.2

Tack, Saartje 37 n.7
Teesside United campaign (Boro Walkers
    Association) 95 n.5
temporal continuity 20
theory of performativity 64
Thompson, Robert 'Mouseman' 81,
    95 n.8
    Robert Thompson's Craftsmen 95 n.8
tide clock 30, 68, 84, 94
Timmermans, Stefan 52, 99
The Troubles (Derry-Londonderry) 9, 72–4,
    77, 94 n.2
Turnbull, Pauline 63

unemployment (UK) 70

verdicts (coroner) 55, 62–3, 100
vernacular memorials 7, 9, 11, 69, 81–5
violence/violent death 51–2, 57, 64, 76–7
von Einsiedel, Orlando
    Evelyn 9, 11, 90–3
    Virunga 91
    The White Helmets 91

wake of suicide 4, 7, 10, 12, 13 n.3, 42, 45,
    87, 91, 93, 102
Warren, Jonathan 70
Wertheimer, Alison 3, 49, 62, 66 n.9
    suicide methods (England and Wales)
    50
White, Jennifer 4, 97
    Critical Suicidology 4
    relationality of suicide 97
witnesses 4, 16–17, 29, 62, 93
wooden memorial benches 81–3, 85, 94
Woods, Angela 5–6
Woolf, Leonard 35, 37 n.9, 45, 48–9
Woolf, Virginia 8–10, 29, 32–3, 37 n.9,
    37 n.10, 45, 48–9, 52, 65 n.6
    On Being Ill 13 n.2
    To the Lighthouse 32
    Modern Fiction 25–6
    Mrs. Dalloway (*see Mrs. Dalloway*
    (Woolf))
    The Waves 32
Work Capability Assessment (WCA) 55,
    66 n.10
World Suicide Prevention Day 70
Worpole, Ken 82. *See also* low-key form of
    contemporary memorialisation

Yiyun Li 48, 89
    Must I Go 65 n.1
    suicide as cliché-land 10, 41–9
    Where Reasons End 42, 65 n.1, 87–8